What people are saying abou

SOUND CHECK

"This is a really engaging book for people serving in local worship teams. Kurtis speaks from the heart, offering practical and pastoral advice for better developing teams. A great resource for the church!"

Tim Hughes, worship leader,
songwriter, Worship Central

"Kurtis Parks is an authentic, passionate Jesus lover. He 'walks the talk,' and in *Sound Check*, he talks about his walk with God with bold transparency. Every leader and believer will find profound insight and inspiration from this book. An easy read filled with hard life lessons that we can all learn from."

Paul Baloche, worship leader, songwriter, author

"Jesus warned us of practicing our righteousness before men to be seen by them, but rather to passionately pursue intimacy with God when no one is looking. *Sound Check* will encourage you toward a lifestyle of authentic worship that practices the presence of God, and equip you to lead from a place of genuine delight in Christ. The church needs you to be the same person on and off the platform, and this book will challenge you to be just that."

Stephen Miller, author of *Worship Leaders,*
We Are Not Rock Stars, worship leader,
and founder of Rooted Network

SOUND CHECK

SOUND
CHECK

How Worship Teams Can
Pursue Authenticity,
Excellence, and Purpose

KURTIS PARKS

David C Cook®

transforming lives together

SOUND CHECK
Published by David C Cook
4050 Lee Vance View
Colorado Springs, CO 80918 U.S.A.

David C Cook U.K., Kingsway Communications
Eastbourne, East Sussex BN23 6NT, England

The graphic circle C logo is a registered trademark of David C Cook.

The website addresses recommended throughout this book are offered as a
resource to you. These websites are not intended in any way to be or imply an
endorsement on the part of David C Cook, nor do we vouch for their content.

Bible credits are listed in the back of this book.
The author has added italics to Scripture quotations for emphasis.

LCCN 2016936066
ISBN 978-0-7814-1463-0
eISBN 978-1-4347-1052-9

The Team: Tim Peterson, Keith Wall, Amy Konyndyk,
Nick Lee, Jack Campbell, Susan Murdock
Cover Design: Jon Middel

Printed in the United States of America
First Edition 2016

1 2 3 4 5 6 7 8 9 10

061616

To my wife, Sarah. Thank you for sticking by my side through the early years and running next to me in these present years! Your constant care, compassion, and love have been an anchor for me as I've written my heart onto these pages. You truly are the best demonstration of Jesus's love I know. This book wouldn't have happened without you believing in me, and loving me through the chaos.

CONTENTS

FOREWORD

In the summer of 2009, I sat out on the patio of Ebenezers coffee-house on Capitol Hill with a young worship leader who had just finished leading worship for our Saturday night service. I spotted unique potential, so much potential that I asked him if he'd come and serve at National Community Church.

In the six years that I've known Kurtis Parks, or as I like to call him, KP, I can't say that I've met a more anointed, humble, or gifted worship leader. But it isn't his talent that really sets him apart; it's his desire for the presence of God. I want to be around people who push me, stretch me spiritually. KP is one of those people in my life.

I've learned through the years that worship is a place where heaven touches earth. Something supernatural happens when we stop focusing on what's wrong with us and start focusing on what's right with God. Here's what I know for sure: no one can worship

God like you or for you! Singing is something we do with our mouths, but worship is something we do with our hearts. And that's what God is after, our hearts.

KP has been our worship director at NCC for five years, and there's been a heart shift in our church because of it. There is a stronger desire to get into God's presence. What really impresses me about the way KP leads NCC Worship is that it doesn't just start and end with music. It goes much further than that. While he's an incredibly gifted songwriter and skilled musician, it's his understanding of Scripture and sensitivity to the Holy Spirit's leading that moves our worship services in the right direction. Every time Kurtis has a word to share with me personally, with our team in a staff meeting, or with our church during our times of worship, I lean in a little closer. I believe that those who know God the best are the ones who spend the most time with Him, and I've known KP to be a man who spends some serious time with the Father.

Sound Check is a timely message for this day and age. I believe this book will challenge you to know God in a more genuine way and to lead out of an authentic walk with Jesus. We've never had a greater need for authenticity in this world, and it starts with the church becoming the real deal. *Sound Check* will cause you to examine those areas of your life that you thought were inconsequential, as it dares you to put your heart under the microscope.

As KP shares his personal journey, you'll discover some takeaways that you and your worship team can apply to the way you live and the way you lead. My prayer is that *Sound Check* ignites a movement of true worship that awakens the church, inspires our generation to live with purpose, and reaches a world that is desperate for authenticity!

Mark Batterson
Lead pastor of National Community Church
New York Times bestselling author of *The Circle Maker*

ACKNOWLEDGMENTS

I have to say a huge thank-you to Verne Kenney, Tim Peterson, and the crew at David C Cook for taking a risk on a young worship leader to tell the story of authenticity from what God has done in my life. Although I've written thousands of songs, most of which won't make it out of my basement, this is my first book. I had no idea it would be such a journey. Thanks for your patience and dedication to making *Sound Check* the best it could be! The entire team of editors definitely helped "check" this book, and got out all the feedback and unnecessary noise! Beyond just belief, you have poured your wisdom, knowledge, and heart into me, throughout this process. I'm forever grateful.

Thanks to my pastor, Mark Batterson, not only for being the greatest leader I've ever had the privilege of serving alongside, but also for being one of the most incredible examples of Christ I've ever known. You gave me the drive to do this thing, and I can't imagine having someone better in my corner. You build my faith every time you open your mouth to speak. You never run out of encouragement!

Thanks to Heather Zempel for being my writing coach through this. It's an honor to be on your team doing ministry, and your wisdom, understanding, and guidance will stick with me until the day I stop singing (and breathing). Your office door was always open, which usually meant I was walking through it! Thanks for everything.

I have to give props to my NCC Worship crew. You guys are the best team to do ministry with, and obviously half of my stories come from the paths that we've walked! Chris, Joel, Dan, Carolina, I can't imagine my life being as complete without knowing you all. Thanks for putting up with me and pushing me to be a better worship leader. Love you guys for life!

I'm incredibly grateful to all the pastors and staff at National Community Church! All of the coffee meetings, conversations, and hangouts through the years have inspired me in more ways than I can count. Pastor Dave, you were the first dude I met in DC, and I'll never forget the first time you showed me how to "parallel park" in the city. More than that, our conversations at 7th Street always leave me full and wanting to know Jesus more. I could fill the next hundred pages with more stories from serving alongside this incredibly humble group of Christ followers.

Thanks to all of the worship leaders, pastors, and friends who have mentored me over the past fifteen years. Pastor Danny Chambers, you showed me what a true worshipper was! Chris Estes, you taught me the lesson of hard work paying off. Malcolm Du Plessis, our countless conversations always leave me excited for what's to come. Steph Hasler, you showed me the ropes of Multi-Site, and

I'm still trying to figure it out! Jordan, Josh, and Jason, you guys are my bandmates for life, and I'll never forget our adventures on the road, many of which inspired this book! Elliott, thanks for being my best friend and always answering a call, text, or email. Your walk with Christ has been an inspiration. John Hartley, you are truly my Uncle Johnny! Thanks for always pushing me to be better, and for opening so many doors.

I have a huge debt of gratitude for my Integrity Family. Adrian Thompson, your Irish banter and massive smile always cheer me up. Thanks for never letting me settle and for always challenging me to go to the next level! Mike Murray, you are the consummate pro. I'm grateful that you always want to see me grow and that you're patient when I constantly push back.

I'm so grateful for the best family on the planet. Thanks to my parents, who made me take piano lessons when all I wanted to do was build tree forts in the woods. I don't know if I could've made fort building into a profession, but music has taken me places I never would've imagined. Thanks, Dad, for being a guiding voice in my life and for always having the right words to say. Thanks, Mom, for always having an open door and an open heart. You're always there and it means a lot. Nate and Bethany, you two are the craziest and most awesome siblings I could ask for. Lorrie, you're one of the kindest people I know, and I'm glad you're in my life. Christie, thanks for putting up with my brother and being a great sister-in-law!

Thanks to my better half, Sarah. You know this book wouldn't have happened without you in my corner. You're the best wife and friend that God could've put in my life. You're an amazing mother to our kids, and I see Jesus every time I look at you. Even though Moses and Norah are too young to read this, I love you guys! You give me too many stories and I wouldn't have half a book without you two to inspire it. Daddy loves ya.

Finally, I wouldn't have a purpose, a life, or a reason to exist without the greatest example of authenticity there is—Jesus Christ. You are the way, the truth, and the life. My prayer is that this book would only point people to You. To know You is to know truth. I pray that this book, and that my life, would bring glory to Your name.

1

CHECK YOURSELF

"You're going to Hollywood!"

Along with more than a hundred thousand other *American Idol* hopefuls who auditioned that year, I wanted to hear that phrase directed at me, just as I'd seen it directed at other musicians on TV many times. That day I was handed a yellow slip of paper, and with one sentence the trajectory of my life changed. For better or worse, I was heading down the path to stardom, or so I thought, and oftentimes that path is a parallel lane with Pride Road. It didn't start with *American Idol*.

I played in bands all throughout my high school years. My first group was a boy band called Dream Come True, which I started in the ninth grade with my two best friends. We thought we were destined to become the next Backstreet Boys, but our band pretty much started and ended with a cassette tape recording of what might be the worst song ever written. I can't even remember the title, but we mostly just harmonized to "ooh" and "yeah, baby" over and over. And I'm positive a Casio keyboard was involved at some point. This was before the Casio keyboard drum machines were considered "vintage cool."

My next band, a little more serious, won our high school talent show. After that victory, I decided I wanted to sing and write music for a living. It's another world when you're on stage, all eyes on you, and if you happen to have a talent, people will praise you. All of us want to be entertained, and for those of us who have the performer gene, we want to be the ones doing the entertaining. In college, that fire was fueled even more when I started a rock band called Temple. We played every local dive, frat party, and coffeehouse that would give us a gig.

At this point, it might be important to mention that during all of these "rock star" ambitions—from my early teenage years till my audition with *American Idol*—I was also leading worship every Sunday in a local church. Talk about an identity crisis. Trust me, you can't separate the two walks of life. You'll carry a little bit of church when you play a gig in a bar, and you'll carry a piece of the "rock star" mentality when you're leading people in worship. The more I led worship and the more I played rock band gigs, the more those two roles grew and became increasingly confused. And when you have one foot in each of those worlds, you end up going in circles.

It all led to my brother, Nate, daring me to audition for America's favorite singing competition the summer after I graduated from college. I didn't have much to lose, so I thought, *Why not?* In all honesty, I didn't expect to make it. I knew I could sing in tune, and I definitely didn't lack in the confidence department. I'd sung solos in choir and was the lead singer of some pretty awesome Creed cover bands in high school (I wish I was joking about that one).

But the moment I walked into the DC Convention Center and laid eyes on the twenty-two thousand "Idol" hopefuls, I didn't feel so confident. Trust me, there were far more talented singers in that room than me. But wherever my vocals might've failed, my crazy personality must have shined through, and somehow I found myself making it through to Hollywood. That led to one of the craziest weeks of my life, complete with cameras in my face 24-7. By the end of "Hollywood week," I had made it into the top fifty finalists. However, following the last solo audition round, my journey was cut short when the judges gave me the news that I wouldn't be going on any further. Don't try to Google it—you won't find anything. This was in the era before YouTube, thank God.

I thought I had blown it. I had ruined my big chance to be somebody. Of course, I told everyone in my life that I thought this was the platform God was giving me to spread His message, when all along I used that rationale to disguise the real story—that I wanted to be a famous singer praised by millions of adoring fans everywhere. I remember having a very real conversation with my dad on the night I was dismissed from the show. He said, "Kurtis, if this isn't what God has for you, just wait and see what He *does* have for you."

So I boarded a plane back to Virginia with a renewed sense of hope ... and a new plan for how to make it big. I wish I could say this was the moment when I went into a season of prayer and seeking God's face, to discover His plan for my life. But I can't.

I started my next band, originally named The Kurtis Parks Band, and played as many shows as I could book, squeezing every ounce of exposure out of my short-lived TV experience. This is also the point where I stopped leading worship in the local church to give 100 percent of my efforts toward becoming the next big thing in the pop-rock music universe. I look back on this time of my life and realize that's when pride really started to take ownership of my heart.

"You're going to Hollywood."

That yellow sheet of paper might as well have been the pink slip to my purpose. And I nearly let it slip away.

CHECK YOUR PRIDE

We all want to be real. We want to be the best and most accurate versions of ourselves that God created us to be—authentic, purpose-driven world changers. We weren't placed here by accident, and the gifts we all possess are not design flaws. My prayer and hope in writing this book and sharing my story is to show that we are all in process. As long as we're on this side of eternity, none of us will make it to complete perfection. The good news is, that's not the goal. Where we're going in life isn't nearly as important as *who* we're becoming.

In my own journey, I've tried so hard to be perfect and project an image that I have it all together, all the time. From the stage, that burden just magnifies over time, until we hit the point of collapse. My week was filled with six days and twenty-one hours of struggle, hardship, and battles I was fighting—and losing. Then for three hours on a Sunday morning, I put that all aside and picked up a guitar to lead a congregation in songs I wasn't sure I believed myself. I know so many worship leaders and musicians who feel the same pressure. I was a fraud. Instead of being vulnerable and bringing all of my burdens to the foot of the cross, and leading worship out of a genuine heart, I had compartmentalized my life into what I thought people wanted to see.

In this book, I'll talk about the roadblocks to authenticity and those things that so often stand between us and the destiny we have in Christ. We'll explore how wrong motives, big egos, and a hard heart can be enemies of integrity, excellence, and purpose.

I pray that we would desire above all else to live out a walk of authentic love with Jesus. This whole world cries out for authenticity. It's such a rare thing to find these days. We have movies that are put together with more computer-generated graphics than actual physical objects. We have plastic surgery performed countless times each week. We have more quick-fix, self-help books on the shelves than ever before, mostly showing us how to solve permanent problems with temporary solutions. Every time we turn on the news, we can see another scandal coming to light, and people we thought were the real deal are exposed by the truth of a harsh reality. Lord, help us live authentic lives of worship that would show this world a better way of living. As worship leaders, I pray we will lead the way to authenticity. I pray that the songs we sing are the prayers of our hearts. I pray that we could take off every mask we've made for ourselves, by turning our pride into praise.

It's the battle every believer goes through. Whether it's blatantly obvious or completely hidden, we all deal with the monstrous dragon.

Pride. She'll creep up on you and consume your thoughts. The moment you think you've got her beat is the moment she's already claimed you. The root of all insecurity is a pride issue.

For a time, I led worship at a church whose motto was "Go where you're celebrated, not tolerated." While the intent was to show people they were appreciated, this was a dangerous statement because it told people (especially artists) they needed celebration. Celebration is closely related to glory, and we're in trouble when we take any amount of glory away from the Lord. Considering that all of us were created to worship, it can be dangerously easy to turn praise into pride. In the Westminster Shorter Catechism, we read, "Man's chief end is to glorify God and to enjoy Him forever." That can't happen when we're slaves to our own pride.

Egotism and overconfidence aren't the only forms of pride we must be concerned about. False humility is a slightly less obvious form of pride, and it clothes itself in the same robes that the Pharisees and Sadducees wore in Jesus's day. It is the kind that says, "Oh, praise God, it's all about Him," but inside you shout, "Thank you for finally recognizing my amazing talents!" Let's not pretend to be more humble than we really are. Take the compliment. It's okay. Know that every good gift comes from our heavenly Father and every ounce of glory belongs to Him. We can honor God with our gifts while still being real with people.

Walking with humility is no easy task. In fact, it's counterintuitive to everything this world screams at us. That's how most things tend to work in the kingdom of God, though. Matthew 20:16 tells us, "The last will be first, and the first will be last." And in Luke 14, Jesus says that "those who exalt themselves will be humbled, and those who humble themselves will be exalted." But perhaps the verse that should give us the biggest need for a sound check on pride is James 4:6. It teaches us that God opposes the proud and shows favor to the humble. One thing I know is that I want *everything* I do to have God's hand, His favor, on it. And that just doesn't happen with a prideful person.

Think about someone in your life right now who you would say has a pride problem. Are you rooting for that person? Would you want him or her on your team, in your circle, or on your staff? Probably not. Funny thing is, this same principle even works in non-Christian culture. More often than not, we see people in the spotlight who help others and put the needs of the less fortunate above their own. I'm a huge pro football fan, and I always look forward to those halftime stories of players bettering their communities and serving those around them. They even have a "Man of the Year" award for it! Not too shabby, NFL.

If you want to have God's favor in your life, walk humbly. If you want God on your side, walk humbly. As followers of Jesus, there are so many things that we can think we're doing for God and for His glory, but in reality we are puffing ourselves up in pride and doing things for our own accolades. When *praise* says "for His glory," *pride* says "for my glory."

Every musician, whether a believer or not, deals with pride. As a worship leader, you always hope that it's something you've conquered, but pride can rear its ugly head and take over every time someone tells you, "Awesome service today" or "Great new song!"

Take a look at the life of David—quite possibly the quintessential standard for worship leaders, right? We see him wrestle with the same thing. Pride is a force that fights against the spirit of humility that Christ calls us all to walk in. We know we have to die to pride, so why is it so hard to conquer? It's hardest to overcome when we are finding our affirmation in the words of man instead of the words of God. We long for words to build our esteem. We get a high off it, but the feeling wears off. Proverbs 16 says pride leads to destruction, and that's exactly what happens with so many leaders and musicians when they let it get out of hand. When we crave the shouts of an audience over the whisper of the Holy Spirit, we're missing it. *The applause of man lasts a moment, but the love of God lasts a lifetime.*

The book of James tells us, "Humble yourselves before the Lord, and he will lift you up" (4:10). That's a tough lesson to learn. I know, because I've tried dozens of times to lift myself up and build things for my own good, only to see those things crumble. Every success comes from God's goodness and grace, but we lose our way when we take our eyes off Christ and focus on success. When we walk in humility and let God do the heavy lifting, things tend to go much smoother. With our eyes on Him, He often pours out His blessing, because it's not the blessing we're seeking; it's Him. Seek His face, and He will open His hands.

We call the things of the Spirit "supernatural" because they are beyond our natural way of understanding and seeing things. After reading and taking the test in Gary Chapman's book *The Five Love Languages*, I recognized that the language right at the top for me— next to physical touch (I'm a hugger)—was words of affirmation. God has an amazing sense of humor and paired me up with my wife, Sarah, who has the exact reverse order of love languages as mine. I guess Paula Abdul had it right when she sang "opposites attract." I've since come to realize that an unhealthy need for words of affirmation is closely related to a problem with pride.

There's nothing inherently wrong with the need for affirmation. In fact, God designed us with that very desire, because it can only be fulfilled in Him. Until we find complete affirmation in who God says we are in Christ Jesus, we'll never truly walk in the identity He's given us. Whether I was leading worship in a church or playing a gig with my band, I needed that affirmation. The applause after every song, the lines of people waiting for an autograph, the college girls waiting to talk to me—it was never enough. And when I was leading worship, I knew I was in a dangerous place when I directly correlated people raising their hands in worship to my leading the songs well enough. I started to aim for an emotional response rather than a spiritual awakening.

We see most heroes in the Bible at some point come face to face with their pride. Moses thought he could do everything by himself until his father-in-law, Jethro, gave him some life-saving advice—that he needed other people to help and share the leadership load. It was pride that led David to commit adultery, and it was pride that caused the disciples to argue over who would be greatest in the kingdom (right in front of Jesus!).

In his book *Mere Christianity*, C. S. Lewis called pride "the great sin." He wrote, "It is Pride which has been the chief cause of misery in every nation and every family since the world began." We can't afford to let any ounce of pride creep into our worship spaces. So how do we attack it?

CHECK YOUR EGO

My first official rock tour was back in 2005 with my band The Season. We had booked about twenty-five shows in a monthlong stretch and were excited to get out on the open road in our tour bus. Okay, maybe it wasn't so much a tour bus as a 1997 Ford Econoline conversion van, fully equipped with a foldout couch bed in the back and track lighting all along the interior. Oh yeah, we were a big deal.

Most people have a glamorous vision of what it's like to tour with a rock band. But the truth is, most nights we crashed on couches and floors. We ate peanut-butter-and-jelly sandwiches until our taste buds could no longer tell the difference between white and wheat bread. Nevertheless, we were ready to get out to every music venue, coffee-house, dive, and street corner we could book and rock the music we'd been working on for months in the studio.

The last show on our first tour was in our guitar player Josh's hometown, Richmond, Virginia, at one of the most famous rock clubs on the East Coast. This was about our twentieth show that month, so by this time we were pretty sure we were experts and going to be the next big thing to hit the pop-rock music scene. I led most of our songs from piano, but we had one song where I was able to walk around and get the crowd hyped. However, this particular night I decided to stand up on my piano bench and, from four feet high in the air, get the crowd clapping to the beat. It was going great until one of the bolts came loose in the bench, and I literally had about two seconds in the air when my feet were higher than my head. That night, the proverb "Pride goes before destruction, and a haughty spirit before a fall" became a reality.

Pride is one of the biggest enemies of an artist's calling. And for worship leaders, it can be a devastating chain that drags you to the lowest valleys.

I hope that as I'm writing this, and as you're reading this, we can each discover some ways to overcome pride, lead worship from a heart of gratitude, and see an authentic move of the Holy Spirit that sweeps over our generation. Authenticity is the key to worship and leading people effectively into the presence of God. When you sound check on stage, you're making sure the sound coming out of the main speakers is the most accurate representation of what you're playing. You weed out the feedback, identify what volumes need to be raised or lowered, and get a true overall mix of what's on stage. When we sound check our hearts, we identify the areas in our lives that need to be adjusted.

I'll be honest and say that some of this book will seem a little ADD (which I struggle with). Welcome to my world—or I should say welcome to my wife's world. I'm sure there's a support group out there somewhere for wives of worship leaders, because God knows my wife deserves a medal of honor. In fact, it was really her patience and prayer that got me to return to my first passion of leading worship after years of chasing a pipe dream to be a rock star.

After starting The Kurtis Parks Band, I sent my album out to every producer I could get an address for, and I heard back from only one, Chris Estes. He was one of the first people, other than Mom and Dad, who really believed I had a gift for music. Together with my wife and a couple of music buddies, the band moved to Nashville to start our journey as The Season. We had some amazing times, and I could tell you stories on end that would have you laughing, crying, and questioning the meaning of life. But that would turn this into an autobiography, and no one wants to read that. We played hundreds of shows, all across the United States, and it all led to a night in the fall of 2008, when I would have a talk with my small-group leader, Chad Usherwood. That conversation would change the course of my life.

You see, my band had just been offered an epic TV contract to go on a show that would no doubt make us a household name: *America's*

Got Talent. Everything in me wanted to sign the contract, go on the show, win the competition, and spend the next years in life becoming rich and famous. I tried justifying signing the contract so badly, but something in my spirit couldn't shake the fact that this wasn't the right path to take. This was back at the time the phrase "a God thing" was a big deal. So I tried being superspiritual and saying, "Is this a God thing? Well, those initials are AGT, just like *America's Got Talent!*" I think I was stretching a bit there.

I brought the opportunity to Chad, and after about two hours of talking through the positives and negatives, he asked me point blank *the* question: "Kurtis, are you here to make *your* name famous or *God's* name famous?" It broke me. Honestly, if many of us would ask ourselves that very question and answer it, we'd find out more about ourselves than any online quiz could ever reveal.

I knew in that moment what I had to do. I had to choose destiny over desire. I had to say good-bye to my earthly passions and say hello to my eternal calling. I knew signing that TV contract would be signing a spiritual death warrant. A battle raged between my ego and my spirit, and my spirit had the upper hand for a change.

It was honestly one of the first times I *didn't* let my ambition overtake the still, small voice that was whispering the Holy Spirit's direction. I remember telling the executive producer of the television show over the phone that we'd have to pass on the offer. There was complete silence for about ten seconds until he said, "Are you sure about this?" I had never felt surer, or crazier, in my life. I look back on that phone call and see it as a round in the boxing ring with my pride. And I had won. It's a daily fight, and unfortunately, I don't win every round. Up until that night's conversation, I had envisioned being in my own tour bus listening to my own songs on the radio, while dragging my family to stadiums packed with people screaming my name.

Lots of "me" and "my" in that dream, right? When we pick up God's dream for our lives and lay down our selfish ambitions, we begin to think with an eternal mind-set. When we stop chasing fame, we're able to start building legacy. We need worship leaders less concerned with making a name and more concerned about leaving a legacy. It's beautiful when you realize that the things of this world will fade away, because it actually frees you to focus on the things of eternity.

I have to constantly be aware of pride in my life, and I know that the moment I feel I have it beat is the very moment it has me beat. I recently got Micah 6:8 tattooed on my arm as a constant reminder that God honors the humble. In this amazing verse, Micah poses a question that all of us ask at some point in our lives: "What does the Lord require of you?" Then he answers it with three simple ways to live: "Act justly, love mercy, and walk humbly." It's one of the only tattoos I have that faces back at me, reminding me of God's requirement in life. Get those three things right and your life will reflect the very heart and nature of Christ.

CHECK YOUR PULSE

The first car I ever owned was a 1984 Honda CRX. I bought it right when I turned sixteen and paid for it in full with money I had earned working at our local burger shack. I'm not sure what your high school culture was like, but if it was anything like mine, the car you drove determined your cool factor. So I knew what I had to do with my beat-up old Honda. I had to turn it into the next *Fast and the Furious* car-star. This was also right around the time when MTV's *Pimp My Ride* was one of the biggest shows on the network. Since I didn't have Xzibit's phone number, I invested the next $500 I made into a new paint job (school bus yellow) and went to Wal-Mart and bought a pair of plastic alloy rims, which were really just hubcaps you slapped on to make the outside of your tires look like the real deal.

About three months later, because of faulty wiring in my stereo system, my car caught fire and burned up, all the way down to the tire rims. I mean, literally, nothing was left but a smoking frame. I had covered up my car with everything to make it look cool on the outside, but in the end, it all just burned up.

We can have the right appearances as worship leaders, but that doesn't always lead to authentic results. You may have the coolest-looking, most-talented musicians leading songs, but leading songs isn't the same as leading worship. We've overlooked anointing and asked for talent, and in doing so I'm afraid we've created a show instead of an atmosphere where God's Spirit can move. We've elevated production and minimized presence.

Don't get me wrong. I'm so excited about the church at large and where we are heading. We're living in a day and age when the gospel can be advanced at a quicker pace than at any other time in history. People can tweet their testimonies or Facebook their faith. An Instagram video of a powerful baptism in church can capture not only people's attention but also their hearts. Yet in an era when connecting is easier than ever, we've lost the face-to-face value of relationship, and that threatens the church. A worship leader can't learn how to lead worship on YouTube. You can't take a five-day course on ushering in God's presence.

I've never gone to seminary, and someday I honestly hope to have the margin and capacity to do that. I did, however, go to Virginia Tech to study finance and music (Go Hokies!). When it comes to ministry school, I like to say I went to the same Bible college as the disciples did—the school of Holy Spirit Hard Knocks. Here were twelve ordinary dudes, who I dare say learned more in three years walking with Jesus than many scholars do spending decades in a classroom. You can't know God by just reading about Him. You need to walk with Him, listen to Him, and seek Him.

There's a huge value in education, and Scripture says to "study to show yourself approved" (2 Tim. 2:15 KJV). So learn, learn, learn, and put it into practice. Just don't rush it. It's wild to me that it takes four years at a major university to earn a bachelor's degree, and yet when it comes to the responsibility of leading worship, many out there take the stage just because they know how to play an acoustic guitar and sing on pitch.

Envision a scarecrow out in the fields. Although birds and hungry animals may think it's a farmer ready to pounce, in actuality a scarecrow is a lifeless form. It has no heartbeat, and it poses no real threat to a predator. I've been there. We call it going through the motions. Autopilot. A scarecrow on a stage. I've zoned out while leading a song in front of a congregation I was supposed to be leading to the throne. The great thing is, as my pastor Mark Batterson often says, *God moves in spite of us, and not because of us.*

So how do you avoid the autopilot disease? Simple: authenticity. God doesn't need the most-talented, best-looking musicians or songwriters leading worship. He needs people who are authentically chasing after His heart. Scripture tells us the exact kind of worshippers God is interested in: "Yet a time is coming and has now come when the true worshipers will worship the Father in the Spirit and in truth, for they are the kind of worshipers the Father seeks. God is spirit, and his worshipers must worship in the Spirit and in truth" (John 4:23–24).

If you think some worship leader with weird hair, funky shoes, and tattooed arms is the standard, then I'm your guy. But chances are I'm more likely the dude who's been kicked out of your church than the one who has been invited to guest lead. I've been in some wild places, and I've seen some interesting things. Today, I somehow find myself in the worship director role at National Community Church, a multisite church based in Washington, DC, pastored by one of the greatest leaders I've ever met. I know God has a sense of humor because He's placed me in a position that's way out of my league. Don't worry, I tell my team that all the time. But here's the great part. It just means I have to rely on God and get on my hands and knees in prayer for everything. I don't know of anyone in ministry who could do it—do it *well*—without the presence of God. If I'm not in prayer and in the Bible at the start of every day, I can tell. The car next to me in stand-still traffic can tell. My wife can tell. In fact, my wife and the Holy Spirit must have pretty regular phone calls, because they always seem to be on the same page.

Here's the scoop. I never wanted to work at a church. I'm a PK (pastor's kid), and my initials are KP. Not sure why I said that, but it felt right. My dad was an awesome pastor, and I'm really grateful that I wasn't another one of those preacher's kids who turned up on *America's Most Wanted*. I had moments of rebellion, and I had to figure out if my faith was my own or just something I had adopted from my parents. That was my freshman year of college. I'm grateful for the right people around me who invested in me and called me out for being an idiot. I'm grateful that my rebellion was short lived. But even after owning my faith, I had no desire to be a pastor or to be on staff at a church.

I've said before that there have always been the two battling natures within my music life: worship leader versus rock star. But first a little background on how I got into music. I know that God gave me any ability that I have, but I also have to thank my parents for pushing me to steward the talent and pursue my love for music. When I was eleven years old, they enrolled me in piano lessons. My dad told me he knew he was called to plant a church and that when he did, I was going to lead worship. I thought it was a joke until he offered to pay me ten dollars a week to practice an hour a day. Hey, to an eleven-year-old, ten bucks equaled three packs of baseball cards, so I went for it. When I was thirteen, I made the biggest mistake of my childhood by telling Mom and Dad they didn't have to pay me anymore because I loved playing music. Looking back, I could've squeezed at least a couple of hundred more dollars out of my folks.

Sure enough, when I was thirteen, my family moved to Roanoke, Virginia, and my dad started The Rock of Roanoke church. I remember at that stage in life I was listening to a lot of punk music, so I feel really bad for those early church members. They got a lot of three-chord, nasal-toned singing, hard-drum versions of "Open the Eyes of My Heart Lord" and "I Could Sing of Your Love Forever." However, my dad gave me the opportunity to experiment and learn how to lead worship. Knowing how those early worship moments had monumental impact in shaping where I am today, I look back fondly on those days. Side note: If God hasn't yet revealed to you what *your* specific purpose and vision are, then serve someone else's. Back when my dad enrolled his eleven-year-old punk kid in piano lessons, he most likely had no clue that his son would grow up to become a worship director at a church in Washington, DC.

I started writing songs at fourteen, using my dad's sermon notes as fuel for lyrics, foreshadowing how I now write with our gifted team at NCC for every series we do, which usually leads to an album every year. I learned how to run an effective rehearsal in those early three-piece-band days (me on lead acoustic and vocals, my brother on drums, and my uncle on bass). I got to see many of my high school classmates step into church for the first time, several giving their hearts to Jesus through the invitation of music. Now we see dozens of guests every week, across multiple campuses, commit their lives to Jesus, as our worship teams lead songs that turn into soundtracks for our conversations with God. Thanks, Mom and Dad. The piano lessons paid off. Even at ten dollars a week.

CHECK YOUR TIMING

After I moved to Nashville in 2005, our band recorded an album and began to tour. I can remember more than once arriving to a venue late, which usually resulted in our not getting a sound check. Instead, the people in charge would let us quickly plug in and just make sure every instrument and microphone was picking up noise to some extent. That's called a line check. The major difference in a sound check and a line check is time. With a sound check, you get to work out the kinks and ensure that when it comes time to play the music, what the audience (or congregation in a church setting) hears is what you want them to hear. Too often in our worship lives, we settle for a line check—just making sure that some signal is coming out, but not a refined sound. The consequences can be detrimental to your sound, and shocking results can happen. Let me explain.

I learned the hard way that a sound check is *always* necessary. I love Guatemala, and nearly every year over the past five years, I've led a mission trip to the beautiful Central American country, partnering with an incredible organization called Champions in Action. This organization is dedicated to seeing the lives of at-risk youth in Guatemala changed by the power of the gospel through the love of soccer. So whenever we go, I get the opportunity not only to be schooled in soccer by a bunch of twelve-year-olds but also to lead worship (in my half-decent Spanish) at the nightly chapels that are held during the week.

On one particular trip, we were using a PA system that we had never used before and we didn't have time for a proper sound check. We arrived late to the camp, a big storm blew in, and everything ran behind schedule. What is it about lightning that sends 120 teenage campers into a frenzy? So the band did a quick line check, and as the chapel filled with soaking-wet teenagers, we got ready for a night of worship.

Now, I usually sweat when I'm leading worship in an air-conditioned church during winter months, but when I'm in 100 percent humidity in the summer in Guatemala, I look like Kevin Garnett in the fourth quarter of the NBA Finals. And in the middle of one of our songs that night, a drop of sweat connected from my lip to my quickly sound-checked vocal mic and sent a fully visible electric shock that still makes my upper lip twitch. The entire chapel's lights went out! Of course, all the kids freaked out, and after flipping on a decades-old generator, we were able to resume singing worship to the Lord. It was more "frightful" noise than a "joyful" one, but we still worshipped.

In our hurry, we didn't check to make sure that all the cables were properly plugged in and that every single mic was getting the right sound. Because of our haste, I nearly lost my life. Okay, maybe it wasn't *that* dramatic, but it was definitely the scariest moment of my worship-leading life. Hey, when it's my time to go, leading worship isn't a bad option! Take the time to sound check, both your music and your life.

We live in a day and age when we can have what we want, when we want it. Our parents used to take their film rolls to the local store to get photos developed, whereas we have the luxury of not only instantly seeing the pics we take on our phones but editing them with the latest app (and even superimposing kittens on our photos). The instant-gratification lifestyle has taken a toll on our spiritual lives, whether we admit it or not. I'm seriously the most impatient person I know. I pray for patience daily, but after about five minutes of praying and not feeling like I've gotten it, I move on. Okay, I'm exaggerating—but not much.

When my son, Moses, was born, I was completely pumped for at least two big reasons: because he brought so much joy to our house (the kid never stops smiling) … and with each of our children's births, we announced their names to the world, I was allowed to get their names tattooed on me. Tattoos definitely bring their fair share of controversy in the church, but most of mine are scriptures that tell the story God has written throughout my life, and they've opened up a lot of intense conversations about Jesus with people I may have never had the chance to talk to. So there's that. If you don't like tattoos, then you can skip this story, or you can read it, because it's pretty funny, and it's a good illustration of impatience.

The moment we knew we were going to call our son Moses, I went to the drawing board and sketched out a cool tattoo for him. In high school I was a decent artist, whereas these days I can draw a pretty cool stage plot, but that's about it. So I had drawn up the idea and after months of waiting for my appointment to get the ink, the day finally came.

With pinpoint accuracy, my tattoo artist, Brad, drew up the picture I had explained to him. It looked so epic. It had the Red Sea parting and the burning bush, with "Moses" written in ancient English script. In fact, it looked so epic that I didn't even think to double-check the Scripture reference etched at the bottom that tied the whole tattoo together. Exodus 15:2 is the verse we pray over our son—it's his life verse. For the record, my daughter Norah's life verse is Matthew 21:16. I highly recommend parents giving their kids a verse to pray, declare, and prophesy over their lives, because it sheds a whole new light on praying over your kids. So Moses's life verse says, "The LORD is my strength and my song; he has become my salvation. He is my God, and I will praise him, my father's God, and I will exalt him." Pretty amazing verse, but I didn't even notice that the tattoo actually had Exodus 15:12 at the bottom. It might not have been a bad verse to put in the tattoo, but it definitely doesn't pack the same punch. Exodus 15:12: "You stretch out your right hand, and the earth swallows your enemies."

I didn't catch the mistake for two weeks until Mike Whitford, one of NCC's campus pastors, saw my Instagram post of the tattoo and wanted to know the story behind the verse. So of course I launched into this cool story of how we were praying that Moses would be a worshipper who always exalted the Lord and found strength in God, his salvation! The look on Mike's face said it all. But then he actually said, "That ain't what Exodus 15:12 says." I felt like I was about to lose my lunch. Now, I'm happy to say that I've gotten the tattoo fixed, and I do have the correct verse on my arm, but it was a hard lesson to learn in patience. Not to mention, it was a painful lesson.

We've all heard the saying that Rome wasn't built in a day, yet we've seen reality shows where a small group of people can build a beautiful three-story, six-bedroom house in less than a week. If there's one principle throughout all of Scripture that my life has learned the most from, it's the concept of "seed time harvest." That is, plant the seed, let God's timing work things out, and then you'll reap the harvest. In fact, the name of my band The Season came from a message I heard preached on the three seasons of the Word of God over our lives: the season of the Word received, the season of the Word tested, and the season of the Word fulfilled. We get superexcited when the first season happens, because we finally have a promise to hold on to and we get a glimpse of what our specific purpose and calling in this life are. We also obviously love the third season, because that's when it all makes sense. When the Word is fulfilled, we start to live in the harvest and reap the fruit of our labor. It's that darn middle season that none of us really want to find ourselves in—the season of the Word *tested*.

No one really enjoys a test, and by its very nature, a test is not easy to get through. However, we also know that you can't have a testimony without a test. We see from Genesis to Revelation that nothing happens without the test of time. Look at the life of Abraham. He had to wait till he was well past senior-citizen status to become a dad and see God's promise come to pass. Moses circled the wilderness for forty years. Joseph was wrongfully thrown into pits and prisons for thirteen years. And fifteen years separated the time from David's anointing to his taking the throne.

Let's also consider the payoffs in the lives of these men as they stood the test of time to see the promise of the Lord fulfilled. Abraham is known as the father of faith. Moses led the children of Israel to the Promised Land. Joseph became second in command to Pharaoh and saved both Egypt and Israel from famine. And David went down as possibly the greatest king of Israel and the ultimate songwriter in all of Scripture. Nothing that comes easy is ever worth it.

When it comes to leading worship, don't rush it. Enjoy the journey, and learn from every bump in the road. Stay faithful to the course God has called you to run. One of the biggest enemies of authenticity is the "fifteen minutes of fame" syndrome. We are quick to overlook the faithful and glamorize the famous. Think of faithfulness as a crockpot. Pot roast, barbecue pork, and my other favorite dishes are the ones that simmer and marinate all day long. The flavors intensify and the juices are practically running out (mouth watering ensues). Those meals might take a little longer to prepare, but they are well worth the wait. Fame is a fleeting microwave dinner. It puts a horrible taste in God's mouth and leaves us hungry for something real. Those who remain steadfast to the call end up as a sweet taste in God's mouth and esteemed in His eyes. I'd say that's the mark we should all shoot for.

CHECK YOUR ACTIONS

We've all heard it at some point, especially if we were raised in the church: "Act like a Christian!" Any time I was behaving badly or embarrassing my parents, I would hear that phrase. As trivial as it might seem, to some degree hearing that message so many times over the years implants in us the idea that we can put on an act. We can try our hardest to fool everyone around us by making others think we are genuinely living a life that pursues Christ. Maybe we can fool people, but we can't fool God. The One who sees all and knows all isn't interested in an act. He wants to see us truly changed, from the inside out. And when you have real transformation, there's no need to act.

Before moving to DC, I spent five years in Nashville, and it is still one of my favorite places on earth. It has the best barbecue spots, and since it's known as Music City, you'll never lack great bands to check out any night of the week. In my early years in Nashville, my band's manager wanted us to make as many connections as we could by getting out there and "networking." Now, I had never really done this before, but I quickly realized that most new artists and unknown songwriters in a town of big shots know how to put on the act. The right lingo, attire, and attitude can sometimes open the right doors. But I didn't have any of that.

One of my biggest fails in trying to act the part happened early on in my time in Nashville. I got invited to hang out with some really great country musicians. Most of them had toured with well-known artists, and I was definitely the odd one out. After hanging out for a while, everyone picked up instruments, as if a hidden camera was about to capture a music video. They asked if I knew the Nashville

Number System, and I nodded confidently, as if to say, "Of course I do!" Truth was, I thought it was some sort of math equation and had no clue at the time what it involved. I didn't want to be laughed at or thrown out of the cool club, so I just acted natural. Then the group of insanely talented musicians started jamming, calling out where they were going by the numbers, and I just did my best at the piano to play notes that were in the right key. After about fifteen minutes of putting on the charade and probably playing about twelve total notes, it became pretty obvious I had no idea what the Nashville Number System was.

You can act the part, but when it comes time to *react*, the truth will always come out. Actions can be manufactured, but reactions are always genuine. Unfortunately, I never saw that group of musicians again, and hopefully, for my sake, they've forgotten my name by now.

If we want to be the genuine article and lead worship with authenticity, we need to be ready for any situation. That way, we're able to react from a posture of praise. Reading the room and the spiritual temperature of our congregation is a huge part of leading worship. To do that, preparation is key. I love what worship leader and songwriter Paul Baloche says about this. He urges worship teams to "practice, practice, practice, and on Sunday, be prepared to forget it all." Athletes would never expect to get called into the big game by their coach if they hadn't been practicing all week. My brother, Nate, is an incredible athlete who played Division I college baseball, and he can tell you that championships aren't won on the playing field, but on the practice field.

Every musician and singer knows the reality of not preparing for a gig, or when it comes to worship, not preparing for the weekend service. Before having our two kids, my wife was one of the go-to bassists at NCC and played nearly every weekend at our Potomac Yard campus. At the last minute, Sarah was asked to play bass for an all-girl band that one of our worship leaders was putting together for the annual women's conference. However, because it was organized so late, there wasn't time for a rehearsal. Sarah reluctantly agreed to play and learned all of the songs note for note, as they were arranged on the recording. The only problem was, on the morning of the event, the worship leader decided to change several keys and most of the arrangements.

Now, Sarah is no Victor Wooten, but she can lay it down on the bass. Yet with a rushed sound check and a quick run-through of the songs rather than a proper rehearsal, she wasn't too confident about the sound that would come out. So she did what any self-respecting musician would do in that situation—turn the volume knob all the way down and pretend to play. Had there been proper preparation and a quality sound check, maybe they could've had some nice low-end frequencies rocking the house that morning.

My point is this: you don't want to put on an act, prepare your heart, and come ready to bring an offering that you think is worthy to give a King. God's not looking for a cheap replication—He's looking for the real thing. He wants the Abel offering, not the Cain leftovers. As we read in Genesis 4, "Now Abel kept flocks, and Cain worked the soil. In the course of time Cain brought some of the fruits of the soil as an offering to the LORD. And Abel also brought an offering—fat portions from some of the firstborn of his flock. The LORD looked with favor on Abel and his offering, but on Cain and his offering he did not look with favor" (vv. 2–5).

God wants our first, our best, and our all. And He deserves nothing less.

CHECK YOUR MOTIVES

Part of sound checking is taking a pulse of our motivations. Why are we doing what we're doing? Is it for the affirmation of man or for the applause of heaven? In 2013, I had the opportunity to take part in a worship project that included several churches. It was my first time being a part of a major-label release, and I was one of three worship leaders asked to spearhead the songwriting and worship leading for a live album called *One: A Worship Collective*.

We were about a month out from a meeting where we would each share some of the songs we had written, and I was under an enormous amount of stress, feeling like I had to write a "hit song" that would make the album a success. I remember sitting in a seat at a Catalyst conference in the weeks leading up to our meeting. During his session, Pastor Matt Chandler encouraged everyone to take a moment to hear God's voice and to seek His face. In that moment, I heard God whisper a simple question to me: "Would you write a song for Me if I was the only One to hear it?" I lost it. I knew that I had placed this pressure on myself to write a hit song when God was just calling me to obedience and trust in Him. What would it matter if I had a song that changed the world but missed touching the Father's heart? Weeks later, when we all met up in Dallas, it was an amazing time of sharing songs. We even spontaneously wrote a song out of the unity in that room called "To Honor

You," which may be one of my favorite songs I've had the chance to be a part of.

When worship is the real deal, there shouldn't be any stress about it. I know that because 2 Timothy 1:7 tells us, "God has not given us a spirit of fear, but of power and of love and of a sound mind" (NKJV). Where His Spirit is, stress, anxiety, and fear cannot abound. So many times we keep ourselves up at night worrying about the guitar part that wasn't perfect or the lyrics we need to rewrite for the fiftieth time. Authentic worship cultivates an atmosphere of peace. So don't worry.

We must check our motives and attitudes in worship, be honest with ourselves when we get off track, and allow God's love and grace to pull us back into the right heart and mind. I've written how pride is a constant enemy of praise. The two cannot coexist. For me, a sound check—or motive check—is usually a pride check. The moment leading worship, writing songs, and operating in ministry becomes about building my kingdom instead of building Thy kingdom, it's time to pull back. This is one of the main reasons I've been intentional about releasing worship projects under a band name, or more recently our church's name, rather than under my own name. It helps me keep it about the right things, and not about me or what I'm doing.

I'm not saying people who release projects under their own names are doing something wrong. In fact, when motives are right, God will use a person and a name to further His name on the earth. God uses people, plain and simple. And it's amazing that in our ordinary being, He can perform His extraordinary will. He gives platforms, and if you operate in humility, submitting to leadership and to God's Word, He can use you. The apostle Peter says, "In the same way, you who are younger, submit yourselves to your elders. All of you, clothe yourselves with humility toward one another, because, 'God opposes the proud but shows favor to the humble.' Humble yourselves, therefore, under God's mighty hand, that he may lift you up in due time" (1 Pet. 5:5–6).

Walk with one foot in front of the other, in humility and integrity, and allow God to do the exalting in His time. Whether He chooses your ministry to reach thousands or to reach your family, whether He uses your song to bless your home church or the global church, is up to Him. Let your motivation start and end with obedience.

If God tells you to do it, then do it. Let Him open the right doors, if that is part of His plan. Of course, this is not to say that we should be lazy and not steward our gifts and calling. But if this comes at the cost of striving and compromising, then I can guarantee you that is not God's purpose. We have a saying at NCC: "Pray like it depends on God; work like it depends on you." It's not one or the other; it's "both/and." But both in our prayers and in our working, let our motivation be pure.

When I was traveling around with my rock band, I wrote songs with the dream that one day people would be out in the crowd singing those lyrics back to me. Since sound checking my life and my dreams, I now long for the day when people are able to sing songs I write to connect with their Maker. In the rock-band world, I operated with the belief that we had to be our own biggest champion because of the notion that "if you don't promote yourself, then you can be sure no one else will." But the kingdom of God isn't a "survival of the fittest" world. There's room for everyone, and when we all set our eyes above, wanting to see His glory rather than our own, the world can change. May we always promote the name of Jesus over our own.

FOR GROUP DISCUSSION OR
PERSONAL REFLECTION

1. How do we keep *our* dreams in line with God's will?

2. What can you put in your daily life to keep yourself from hitting "autopilot" in your walk with God?

3. What are some of the motives and reasons you got into leading worship?

2

CHECK YOUR SIGHT

Whenever you hear people say they're a "touring musician," that pretty much always means they have some other lame job they work at while not on the road. For me, that was being a food delivery guy. Those jobs come in handy mostly because the schedule is so flexible and you can always get time off with late notice. I worked for a Chicago-style restaurant, delivering deep-dish pizzas and Italian beef sandwiches to people all over the greater Nashville area—that is, when I wasn't busy stuffing my own face with the food. Hopefully, I didn't kill too much of our profit margin.

On one late-night run to a pretty sketchy part of town, I made a routine delivery to an apartment building. When I arrived, a guy standing by a car in a dark area began to rapidly make his way toward me. He kept asking if I needed anything and started walking faster in my direction. All of a sudden, he pulled out a can of mace and unloaded it on me, about six inches from my eyes. I don't know if you have ever had your face covered with pepper spray, but just imagine having the worst sunburn you've ever had—on your eyeballs. Needless to say, I couldn't see a thing.

As I hit the ground, swinging my fists frantically, the thug told me he had a gun and was going to kill me. He demanded all of my tip money, which, unfortunately for him, was mostly just a bunch of signed credit-card slips. I guess he forgot that since the invention of credit-card machines, people rarely pay with cash.

As soon as I started to regain my vision, I quickly got into my car and grabbed the steering wheel. You would think I would've sped off to avoid any further danger, but no. I started spinning doughnuts in the parking lot where this guy still stood, trying to capture a description of his car or his license-plate number. After about ten circles, I decided that if this dude actually did have a gun, he would soon begin shooting. So I drove off, back to the restaurant.

It took at least three days for the effects of the pepper spray to wear off and for me to get my full vision back. Not being able to see in a dark neighborhood with a thug in your face is pretty scary. Not having a vision for the course of your life and for your ministry is even more damaging.

To be an authentic leader, you need to have a vision that directs the course of your leadership. Proverbs 29:18 says, "Where there is no vision, the people perish" (KJV). I love the Bible for what it says, and sometimes I have a little fun and reverse the language because in most cases the opposite of what it says is also true. In this case that means, "Where there is vision, the people find life!" I want the songs I write and the worship services I lead to be life giving, both to our church and to the teams that carry our vision on their shoulders.

CASTING A VISION

When I first came to National Community Church, I was hired as a part-time utility worship leader who could have the flexibility to lead at any campus that had the need on a particular weekend. I had the opportunity to learn under Steph Hasler, who was the worship coordinator at the time. It was in these early years that I learned how a multisite church in movie theaters works. And trust me, there was *a lot* to learn. Steph got married in November 2011 and moved to Berlin with her husband, John, to launch our café, Prachtwerk. The worship director torch was then handed to me to run with, and I remember feeling overwhelmed and downright scared of the role I was about to embrace. But I read Proverbs 29, and since downloading that truth of scripture, I start off every year by casting a vision for our worship teams.

I encourage every worship leader I meet to do the same. When you put a specific vision before your worship team, you put wheels on a car and give your team something to drive. In our first year as a team, our vision was "Play with a standard of excellence." It's a great idea to build a vision out of God's words and not our own thoughts. Every vision statement our team here at NCC Worship leans on is rooted in the unfailing Word of God. When you have Scripture as the foundation of vision, you can't go wrong. Man's words are often opinions, but God's words are fact.

That first vision statement came out of Psalm 33:3, which says to "play skillfully" before the Lord. Built on this mantra, we started holding every campus to higher standards, because I knew the offering we were bringing week in and week out at that time was falling short of what God deserved. We began to have every campus hold weekly rehearsals, drummers started playing to click, vocalists did away with music stands, and so on. Now, I'm not saying every church needs to do this to operate with a standard of excellence. This is just what we were convicted to do, and we still have weekends when we don't hit the mark, but at least the foundation is there.

The following year, our vision statement was "Create a culture of worship." This was based on the calling of the Old Testament Levites, as stated by Moses: "At that time the LORD set apart the tribe of Levi to carry the ark of the covenant of the LORD, to stand before the LORD to minister to him and to pronounce blessings in his name, as they still do today" (Deut. 10:8).

I truly believe that to create a culture of worship in your church, you need to have authentic worship leaders paving the path. This charge to the Levites is fundamental to the way we worship today, and this verse has become a go-to recommendation whenever I have the chance to chat with worship leaders. It lays down the proper guidelines for authentic worship. And without guidelines, or rules, you could end up with gummy bears in your pants. Let me explain.

When my brother and I were growing up, nearly every Sunday after church we looked forward to going to one of the greatest restaurant establishments in the country, Golden Corral. It's known for its never-ending, all-you-can-eat lunch buffet. For two teenagers with hollow legs, it was like dangling a carrot in front of a horse.

Now, the sign on the wall said "All you can eat," but it didn't say "All you can eat *here*." So after we had our fill of fried chicken, pot roast, pizza, and hot dogs (yes, those can all be one meal), Nate and

I would line our pockets with napkins. Then we would casually stroll up to the dessert bar and stuff our pockets with as many chocolate-covered raisins, cookies, and gummy bears that we could fit. This was also the main reason we wore cargo pants to church every Sunday. The more pockets, the more gummy bears we could pack in. We made out pretty well. Sadly, we eventually got called on our ploy, and that was the end of the free-for-all at the dessert aisle. My point is, rules are important. America's best buffet restaurant now has a strict policy so customers can't walk out with dessert stuffed into their cargo pants.

You see, Deuteronomy 10 was laying down the ground rules for authentic worship in the tabernacle. The very fact that the verse ends with the phrase "to this day" shows us that we need to pay attention. The Spirit of God inspired that scripture to be written thousands of years ago, and amazingly, it's able to connect with humanity today in our vastly different culture. The three-part calling starts with carrying the ark of the covenant, which was a representation of God's presence in Moses's day. The Levites were called to carry it, which translates to us as worshippers—we're called to carry God's presence wherever we go. One of my prayers is that wherever I go, I will exhibit God's presence.

The second part of the passage tells us to minister unto the Lord. How many times can we lead worship and completely miss the opportunity to minister to our God? We often get so consumed with everything else in worship (keeping the band on task, getting the lyrics loaded into ProPresenter, making sure our hair looks good) that we forget one of the most amazing and intimate goals of worship. I love moments in singing and praising God that are so authentic you

literally forget there's anyone else in the room. That's called ministering to the Lord!

Third, Deuteronomy 10:8 has a call that we can't miss—to bless
in His name. This is where we bless and affirm others around us in
the love, hope, and grace of Jesus Christ. I believe worship is a gift *to*
God, but *for* people. We need to make sure there's a healthy balance
of songs that honor God and minister to Him as well as songs that
declare to the church who we are in Christ.

Based on this vision of creating a culture, our worship team
asked ourselves, "How do we get our church to think of worship as
more than just a warm-up to the message? How do we help people
realize that the closing song isn't just exit music or a cue to go pick
up your kids? It's a chance to respond to God's love." So we began to
write songs that dove headfirst into the Levitical approach to worship
and songs telling us who we were as the bride of Christ. We created
an album based on Romans 8 titled *More Than Conquerors*. We also
challenged the idea that worship is just a set of songs you sing at
a church service. Throughout the year, we held nights of worship
from people's homes—simply called Living Room Sessions—and
broadcast them through our website. Small groups in our church
and friends from all around the country tuned in to worship with
us from their houses. We found out a year later, when we brought
on Carolina Soto as a worship protégé, that she had watched one
of these Living Room Sessions from her hospital bed as she battled
cancer. She said being able to worship that night with us was a huge
encouragement in her fight. Our hope and prayer with these nights
was to show our church that even without the lights, sound system,
and lyrics on a screen, you can worship God from wherever you are.

If you read on a little further in Deuteronomy 10, it goes on to say that the Levites were to have no share in the property claims that the other eleven tribes took part in. In the days of marching into the Promised Land and dividing up territories, the Levites were set apart from bickering over land. The scripture lays out a far better inheritance for the early tabernacle caretakers: the Lord Himself (v. 9). As modern-day Levites, we share in that legacy—that God and His never-failing presence is our inheritance. His presence is our promise.

The next year, our vision was centered on "Becoming a Community of Worshippers." This was based on 1 Peter 2:9, which says, "But you are a chosen people, a royal priesthood, a holy nation, God's special possession, that you may declare the praises of him who called you out of darkness into his wonderful light."

We're called into a relationship with God as well as into community with one another. God didn't just make Adam, wipe His hands, and say, "Cool, I'm good with that!" When God brought Eve into the world, out of Adam's side, He created the essence of community. I'm sure Jesus could've easily become the Savior of the world as a one-man show, but He didn't do it that way. He walked the earth in community with His disciples and left the heritage of the church in His followers' hands.

We are members of a royal priesthood. What an amazing calling we have! We have access to the throne of grace at any time, whereas the Old Testament era had one day a year, the Day of Atonement, and only the High Priest could enter the Holy of Holies. When Christ endured the cross, He tore the veil. He removed any and all barriers that stood between Him and us. So as a worship team, we started placing more value on what it meant to walk as a community of worshippers. We started hosting team nights and small groups, becoming more intentional to create time to grow as a family, outside the music setting. From there, we started to see so much life and authentic love for one another permeate our church.

Our vision for this year is "Only Servants." It's rooted in 1 Corinthians 4:1, where Paul writes, "This, then, is how you ought to regard us: as servants of Christ and as those entrusted with the mysteries God has revealed." This term "servants" actually refers to the under-rowers in the hull of a ship. I'm sure you've seen a pirate movie or two, and there's always a scene with the crew busting their butts to row the ship from below the deck. They're unseen and probably unappreciated, but without them, the ship wouldn't move.

This point is worth repeating: pride is one of the deadly attacks of Satan on any worship leader. We often confuse a platform with a pedestal. God will give us a platform, but people will put us on a pedestal. Pride is the very opposite nature of a servant. One way to overcome the desire of the spotlight is by being unseen. You might take a week and serve on the other side of the mixing board with the production team. I love telling our worship team that we are an extension of the hospitality team. At our Potomac Yard campus, our worship team used to be the greeters when people entered theater 9. Most ministry that we do won't take place on a stage. We need to always point to Christ in everything we do. We must remember that, at the end of the day, we are all only servants.

The statements I've mentioned are all yearly vision casts that happen with our worship team at NCC. However, every yearly vision theme just points back to our overarching vision. Our vision statement is something that all of our worship staff members have on their email signatures, it's on our website, and I bet most of our team members could recite it: "Global revival through personal worship." That's a bold statement. A God-centered vision has to be. It's got to be something that's impossible without divine intervention. If you can make it happen without His help, then it might not have heavenly impact. But if it's something we can do only with God's hand, then it's something only He can get the glory for.

Vision is one thing you'll never run out of if you're spending time with God. In a healthy church, it's something that's demonstrated from the top down. It takes only about two minutes of sitting with Pastor Mark to catch his vision for NCC. Every one of our department heads and campus pastors has that same itch for casting vision within our spheres of influence. I love the fact that Diana Fang, our worship team admin, asks me about twenty times what my vision is going into every team night, worship retreat, and prepping for each album. Of course, there's the fact that it probably takes twenty times asking me a question to sometimes get a response. Did I mention the ADD thing before?

You can never have too much vision, just like you can never have too much of God. Jeremiah 29:13 says that when you seek God with your whole heart, you will find Him. And when you do, He shares with you the secrets of His heart. Finding Him leads to catching a vision for your life, for your family, for your team, and for your church.

When you have that vision from the Lord, it's absolutely critical to write it down. I may not ever know the proper way to say "Habakkuk," but I love what he says in the second verse of his second chapter: "And the Lord answered me, Write the vision, make it plain on tablets, so he may run who reads it" (ESV). I've actually woken up from dreams, grabbed my phone, and jotted things down in my notepad so that I wouldn't forget them later. Some of my best (and weirdest) songs have come from dreams. When you write something down, you can literally say "I have it in writing" and hold yourself accountable to the things God has spoken to you. Vision is a great filter to run all of your big decisions through. It's a lens to help you see clearer. If there's an idea that doesn't line up with the vision, don't do it. Simple as that. This is one of the main reasons I will never record an *NSYNC cover album. It doesn't line up with my vision. Sorry, Justin.

We all need to know our God-given visions. You may think every worship leader has the same vision—to usher people into God's presence. And that's true. As those who are leading our churches in times of praise and worship, we should have the ultimate goal of seeing God's people and His presence connect. But I also believe when we ask God to show us the specifics of who we are as individuals, according to how He's wired us, we'll begin to find our unique purposes. We'll begin to get vision.

Ultimately, your vision may be just that—*your vision* and no one else's. And that's okay. But share it. Leaders are called to challenge and inspire. No one wants to follow people who don't know where they're going.

FOR GROUP DISCUSSION OR PERSONAL REFLECTION

1. Come up with a vision statement for you and your team.

2. Dissect Deuteronomy 10:8. How are you living out the three-part calling of a Levite?

3. When was the last time you simply "ministered before the Lord"? Identify some opportunities where you think you could do this on a regular basis.

3

CHECK YOUR PRIORITIES

In the summer of 2009, I had the chance to travel around full time leading worship at churches, camps, and conferences all over the East Coast. It was the first time I had toured without a rock band. I was pretty much rediscovering who I was, not only as an artist and songwriter, but as a child of God, created to worship.

For about eight weeks that summer, I led worship at Watermarks Camp just outside of Charlottesville, Virginia. Each week, a group of different middle school and high school kids would come in, and the prayer of the staff was to give them a life-changing week of encountering God. Days were filled with fun outdoor activities and awesome camp food (don't ask me what "mystery meat" is), and in the evenings we had chapel, during which I would lead worship with the band. Following worship, a youth pastor or camp counselor would share a message.

On one of these hot summer nights, the power decided to go out in the chapel just minutes before the start of the evening service. I wasn't sure how we were going to do our worship set of mostly synth- and electric-guitar-driven songs. So I had a quick chat with Kris Clifford, the youth pastor scheduled to speak that night, and we decided just to have a stripped-down, acoustic time of worship. Well, I guess the decision was kind of made for us, because of the power failure. We circled all the chairs around the room, and together with Josh, my guitar-slaying band mate, we played two acoustics and sang a few worship songs as loud as we could, hoping the kids would engage. This also happened to be during a week that had the most distant group of kids of the entire summer. Some contraband had been found in a few campers' cabins, and they were totally unengaged in every chapel earlier that week. They didn't even laugh at the "No Purpling" talk we gave. You know, boys are blue, girls are red ... no, you haven't heard it? It's a youth group thing. Regardless, something wasn't clicking this week. But on this particular night, with no PA system, no lighting rig, and no lyrics on a screen, something was different.

Kris began to share his testimony, and for the first time that week, the kids didn't tune out. Toward the end of his message, Kris called me up next to him and asked me to start playing whatever God put on my heart. He mentioned the word *allelujah*, so I began to play and sing the words, "Allelujah, You are God." It wasn't anything magical, but it was a moment that was completely stripped down, simple, and vulnerable. It was a moment when the presence of God was undeniable, and almost tangible. The kids' detached attitudes and hard hearts toward God broke that night, and more hands than we could count went up as Kris asked if anyone wanted to surrender his or her life to Christ. It was one of the most powerful and real moments of worship I'd ever experienced. *When God's presence shows up, you don't have to manufacture a thing.*

That night, I realized that authenticity sometimes comes through strongest when all of your plans fall through. When all of your comforts disappear and things that you set up to succeed wind up failing, whatever comes from what's left, that's who you are. That's the authentic representation of worship that I believe we sometimes miss out on when we're more concerned with putting on a good show than experiencing God's presence.

I later wrote the song "Allelujah" out of that night, and to this day whenever I lead that song, it takes me back to that night at camp.

KNOW HIS PRESENCE

Depending on what your church background is, you probably have different thoughts about what exactly God's "presence" means. So, coming from a biblical standpoint, I'll try to explain what I understand it to mean.

There are two facets to God's presence: omnipresence and manifest presence. God is omnipresent, which means He is everywhere—in the air, in our cars, in the forest, in the city. God is all around us. We cannot go anywhere that He isn't. This is the type of presence you can totally feel if you've ever walked through the woods after snowfall or buried your toes in the sand while staring out at the ocean. There's a special peace we can connect with in God's omnipresence.

Then there is God's manifest presence. While omnipresence says "Wherever we go, there He is," manifest presence says "Wherever He goes, there I want to be!" In Psalm 139, David writes of God's omnipresence when he says, "Where can I go from your Spirit, where can I flee from your presence?" (v. 7). Elsewhere, Moses pointed out the distinguishing factor that God's manifest presence is something to be pursued (Exod. 33:15). This presence is not something we stumble upon, but passionately seek after. "Then Moses said to him, 'If your Presence does not go with us, do not send us up from here.'"

In *The Pursuit of God*, A. W. Tozer wrote, "The Presence and the manifestation of the Presence are not the same. There can be one without the other." Manifest presence is what happened that night at camp. It's when you feel an undeniable, almost tangible connection to God's heart through His Spirit. It's not an emotional high; it's a spiritual awakening. Maybe you've never had one of these moments. If so, I encourage you to get alone with God. I believe that Jeremiah 29:13 refers to experiencing this manifest presence when you seek God with your whole heart. You'll find Him and know Him. God's presence and the Holy Spirit are not necessarily one and the same, but you usually won't have one without the other.

God's manifest presence is like a hot shower. And I could stand underneath a showerhead spouting hot water all day long. I say that jokingly, but it's actually the truth with my brother, Nate. When we were in high school, we were always running late for school in the morning. That's because he would go in for his morning shower, and fifteen minutes later we'd have to barge into the bathroom because he would literally be lying on the bathtub floor fast asleep with the hot water pouring on top of him. It's a miracle he didn't drown.

It doesn't matter how tired I am or how rough my day has been, I feel so much better when I take a hot shower. I feel revived. God's presence is a place of refreshing. He washes away all the junk in our lives and renews us completely. He speaks to us through the Holy Spirit, and we are able to draw closer to His heart.

You cannot lead and live authentic worship if you're not constantly spending time in God's presence. Whatever you are lacking in your life—whether it's love, joy, peace, or patience—you will find it in God's presence, because that's where His Spirit is. When you read Galatians 5, you see an accurate picture of what you'll find in God's presence: "But the fruit of the Spirit is love, joy, peace, forbearance, kindness, goodness, faithfulness, gentleness and self-control" (vv. 22–23). These are the elements that should become more and more of our makeup as we spend time in God's company and as we get to know the Holy Spirit in a very real and intimate way. And here's the really cool thing: when we know more of who God is, we inevitably find out who we are, because we are made in His image, as Genesis reveals.

I often tell the staff I lead that we can't take people on a weekend to a place we haven't been throughout the week. My wife wouldn't feel very loved if I spent only one day a week in her presence, much less only ninety minutes on a Sunday morning. If I told her I loved her only when I was in a room surrounded by many others, and then I ignored her the rest of the week, she would be the first to say our marriage was a fraud. My wife doesn't want a fake expression of love, one that's displayed exclusively in a sea of people. Neither does God.

As worship leaders, we must constantly find ourselves in pursuit of God's presence, which means we must allow the Holy Spirit to be an active part of our daily journey. The Holy Spirit is the catalyst for change in our lives. In the early church, every single thing those believers put their hands to was prompted by the Holy Spirit. The moving of the Spirit brought nearly three thousand people to an altar call, as recorded in Acts 2. Countless signs and wonders that happened throughout the book of Acts and the rest of the New Testament came after Pentecost. It blows my mind that many church experiences in our modern age can go from start to finish without ever acknowledging the Holy Spirit, and I wonder if we've put our "programs" in place of His "presence" by doing so.

The Holy Spirit is probably the most misunderstood part of the Trinity, simply because of the fact that He is spirit. Because many of us have misunderstood the Holy Spirit, we have said "No, thanks" to His working. By doing so, we have cut off the biggest power source in our lives. We are turning our backs on the very Advocate whom Jesus told us He would send: "But the Helper, the Holy Spirit, whom the Father will send in my name, he will teach you all things and bring to your remembrance all that I have said to you" (John 14:26 ESV).

We need the Holy Spirit. If we want our worship services to be the real deal and God honoring, we need to quit treating the Holy Spirit like the third wheel on a Sunday date. To be authentic worship leaders, we must desire more of the Holy Spirit in our lives instead of getting caught up in the latest fads, searching for the coolest songs, and chasing after the best musicians in our cities. God has everything you'll ever need to carry out your calling, and the Holy Spirit is the biggest helper you could ever have.

I pray that we never substitute talent for anointing. May we never replace presence with production. We need both, and one without the other is like playing a drum set with handcuffs on. You could do it, but it wouldn't be pretty.

By the time we step on stage to lead worship, we should be so full of God's presence that we can't *wait* to pour it out into our church body. We need to be positioned as servants, assisting our congregations by providing an atmosphere where God's presence can take center stage. We need to be magnifying glasses that give people a bigger picture of just how good God is and how marvelous the love of Christ is. If we're not desperate for God, then we're satisfied with ourselves. So we must not only remain hungry and passionate for the move of God in our lives, our families, and our churches, but we must also fulfill that hunger on a daily basis by going to the Holy Spirit buffet line. God's presence is the only thing that can satisfy our every need. If we don't run to God for our satisfaction, we start to experience an exhausting form of faith in which our output is greater than our input. That leads to stress, anger, and making lots of mistakes, both on stage and off stage.

The input-output principle is one of the biggest reasons I'm not a huge fan of eating crabs. They definitely taste good, but when I spend twenty minutes pounding away on a crab shell to come away with only two ounces of meat, I just don't think it's worth it. The process is messy, leaving you smelling like the inside of a fishing boat. Crab does taste pretty amazing, though.

Look at the life of Jesus in the Gospels, and you can easily see how demanding His schedule was. I don't think any Google calendar could fit the number of ministry events on His list. And everywhere He went, it was bigger than the Beatles showing up, or for those who don't know the Fab Four, let me just say it was bigger than Justin Bieber hitting the scene. Jesus was a phenomenon in the days that He walked the earth. He couldn't go anywhere without crowds recognizing Him, and that led to a lot of output in His ministry. Yet even Jesus knew that without a consistent stream of input, He would be running around as an empty cup without anything to pour out. If the Son of God had to get away to refill Himself for ministry, then how can we have an impactful ministry without a steady refill? As we read in Luke 5:16, "But Jesus often withdrew to lonely places and prayed." The key word is "often."

I want to camp out on that idea of *withdrawing*, which is one of the hardest things for those in ministry to grasp. I admit that the idea of taking a Sabbath is hard for me to make a priority in my life. I have a tough enough time just shutting down and *resting*.

We live in a culture that associates rest with laziness. And we celebrate busyness. We love to let the world know that we're *doing* something, don't we? How many posts on your Facebook wall or tweets on your Twitter page are full of people telling you what they're *doing*? It's as though if you don't post it for people to see, then it didn't really happen. This probably comes from a place of insecurity, wanting some form of affirmation that if we *do* something, then we'll *gain* respect, love, and honor. More people might like us if they can see how much we contribute to society. If we dare to take a Sabbath and rest, then we're afraid we'll miss out on something important. I'm guilty of it. Whenever I have a day off from working at my church "day job," I take those opportunities to book myself up with studio projects, writing sessions, and other random things to fill up what should be my downtime. Then, of course, I *have* to post photos on social media, showing how busy I am! But that's not a true withdrawal. Resting is resting—simple as that. Anything that is considered "work" is *not* Sabbath.

So many verses in Scripture urge us to unplug, hit the reset button, and allow God to fill us. It doesn't matter how good a battery is, or how long it lasts, at some point it will run out of juice and need to be recharged. And just like a car that needs an oil change, if you don't do the regular maintenance at regular intervals, the engine will eventually blow up. Sabbath should be our weekly maintenance. *When you're constantly being refilled, you'll never be empty.* It's not a suggestion—it's a command. Check out these words from Hebrews 4: "There remains, then, a Sabbath-rest for the people of God; for anyone who enters God's rest also rests from their works, just as God did from his. Let us, therefore, make every effort to enter that rest, so that no one will perish by following their example of disobedience" (vv. 9–11).

So what does Sabbath have to do with God's presence? I don't think the two are separate from each other. Rather, they actually work hand in hand. You see, in God's presence there is rest. In God's presence we are refreshed, recharged, filled up, or whatever other terminology you want to use. Resting in God's presence is both active and passive. We actively engage in pursuing Him and worshipping Him, and yet we are able to let His rest and peace wash over us without striving. You can rest and seek at the same time. Psalm 62:5 says to "find rest in God," and according to Matthew 7:7, "Seek and you will find." To find something, you have to search for it, which is an active thing. We want to go after so many things in this world that promise a false sense of security, worth, and respect. But if we would just place God's presence and His kingdom above all that other stuff, then we would get *all* of it.

One time Jesus told His followers, "Seek first his kingdom and his righteousness, and all these things will be given to you as well" (Matt. 6:33). I believe when Jesus says *all these things*, He means *all these things*. No deep theological discussion is needed. Everything that we need is found when we seek Him first. When we get in His presence.

A pastor once told me that those who know God best are those who spend the most time with Him. I want to be known by God as someone who never stops seeking Him. When you look throughout all of Scripture, you see it said of one particular person that He was a man after God's own heart: David. It's no coincidence that David is also known as one of the frontrunners of worship and music in the Bible. He knew the amazing power and value of God's presence in his life. Whether he was going into battle, running from Saul for his life, or repenting of his sins, David always pursued God's presence. For renewal, guidance, and joy, it was his refuge.

I have one primary goal every time I'm privileged to lead worship, and it has become a mission statement: "Through creativity and excellence, we cultivate an atmosphere of intimate worship and passionate praise, where God's presence and His people connect." As worship leaders, we spend a lot of time talking to our teams about excellence and creativity, and you can see both of those in our core values. Those things are awesome, but they aren't the end goal. God's presence is the end, and excellence is the means. I like to say that God's presence is the destination, and creative excellence is a road that can take us there. We know that without the Holy Spirit showing up at a church service, all we've done is play another nice concert.

One of the constant prayers in our worship team is that we would see God move in revival. What better place to be praying for that than in our nation's capitol, where our church is located. We believe in a vision that says "Global revival through personal worship." Imagine a day when everyone in *your* church is personally seeking God and entering into His presence every day. Now dream of a day when *all* those who call themselves Christians seek God with an unquenchable passion—and then act on their faith to show the world what the church was always meant to be. That, my friends, is called *revival*. You can't have revival in a place where God's manifest presence isn't central. Every movement of revival is rooted in God's presence, from the move of the Holy Spirit in the upper room in Acts 1 and 2, to more recent movements such as Azusa Street at the turn of the last century and Brownsville in the 1990s. If we want revival in our hearts, our churches, our cities, our nation, and throughout the world, we need to become desperate for more of God.

KNOW HIS WORD

A huge part of making God central in your life is meditating on His Word. Somehow we've confused the word *meditate* to mean "you need to take a weeklong trip to the beach and do nothing but ponder the Bible." I love what the dictionary has as one of the definitions of *meditate*: "to consider." Job 37:14 says, "Stop and consider God's wonders." As members of a society that breathes busyness, when was the last time we just stopped in the middle of our day and considered God's wonders? We can lead busy lives in a busy world but still find moments to meditate and pause in the stillness of God's presence.

I try to look for moments throughout my day to center myself, to still my heart, focus my mind, and rest in God's good presence. I'll listen to a Bible app as I'm driving in the crazy DC traffic on my way to the office. And trust me, it's a lot harder to make unkind gestures and harbor hostile thoughts toward other drivers when you're listening to the Bible. I sing worship songs in the shower, and I pray in the Spirit as I'm walking from meeting to meeting. I make the effort to do whatever I can to maximize my time and be intentional about keeping God's presence at the forefront of my life.

Not long ago, I put my daughter, Norah, down for bed. She's very particular about her bedtime routine: We have to read three stories—usually one about Jesus, one about Spider-Man, and one about Thomas the Tank Engine (she has diverse taste). Then I tuck her in tightly and put on a kids' worship album. During the first song, I have to sit on the edge of the bed, and then for the next two songs she asks me to lie next to her and scratch her back. Can you say "Diva!"? On this night, I put on the worship CD and sat on the edge of the bed next to my little girl as usual. Matt Redman's classic song "Better Is One Day" came on, and I spent the next four minutes worshipping right there, on a Minnie Mouse bed, thanking God for His presence. It was a powerful moment, and I realized that God will meet us whenever, wherever, as long as we cry out to Him. He longs to be with us. His presence is a beautiful thing.

Have you ever been in a church service and heard someone say, "You know, it says in the Bible _____," and then the person drops a truth bomb without giving the reference for it? That's great that the

Bible says it, but can you tell me where? I'd like to look it up, read it, and meditate on it. Oh yeah, I'd also like to get a little context on the statement. I must have said this myself a couple of million times before getting convicted to know more Scripture. This conviction came while I was at a conference and Aaron Keyes was leading worship. This dude dropped about ten scriptures before going into every song, and if God's Word is a weapon, as Ephesians 6 says, then I'm pretty sure Aaron was packin' heat that day.

In all seriousness, I realized that my lack of Scripture knowledge could result in a lack in my effectiveness as a worship leader. I had a serious deficit of "Bible brain" or "Scripture smarts." When we share the Word of God in a worship setting, we give the songs we sing validation and perhaps deeper meaning. When our congregations understand that they're singing God's promises and not just man's words, it builds faith and inspires hope.

In every worship service I lead, I challenge myself to find at least one moment to share a scripture, even if it's a brief moment *in* a song, leading into a bridge or a chorus. It doesn't need to be a sermon, but when I share a piece of the Bible, it takes the music to another level. God's Word is living and active, according to Hebrews 4:12, and I truly believe that worship is dead without it. I had the chance to sit in on a worship-leader gathering with some of Hillsong's leaders, and Jad Gilles shared a valuable thought with us: "The people of God will always rally behind Scripture."

Challenge yourself to dive into the meaning behind the songs you're leading. Look up the Scripture passages that inspired them. Give weight to the words you sing. So many times connecting a portion of Scripture to a worship song will make it click with the congregation. I remember leading worship at a gathering of about five hundred small-group and ministry leaders. Before we went in to Matt Redman's song "Wide as the Sky," I shared out of Psalm 63:4: "I will praise you as long as I live, and in your name I will lift up my hands." Immediately, when we went into the verse that says, "Hands up, hearts open wide as the sky," every hand went up into the air as a sign of adoration and surrender to our God. It was one of those powerful moments when I felt like we were mirroring what happens in eternity. That's what worship should feel like—a glimpse of heaven.

If you want to get more familiar with Scripture but don't know where to start, go with Psalms. Every worship leader should treat the Psalms like a playbook for worship. We've got a collection of 150 of Israel's greatest hits.

A couple of years ago, National Community Church presented a nine-week series on Psalms where our teaching team taught on some of the epic psalms, such as 119, 84, and 145, to name a few. Now, our teaching team has some of the most gifted communicators I've ever had the privilege of hearing. They gave the NCC worship team the opportunity to teach one weekend during the Psalms series. We had our work cut out for us, but we definitely took the ball and ran with it. We presented a survey of the Psalms through six TED-style talks, speaking on hard-hitting topics in the book to hopefully give our church a deeper understanding of what musical worship is all about. We also made it a completely interactive service by leading a song after every talk. This allowed people to respond to the Word and make the connection from the message to the music. It challenged us as worship leaders to know God's Word and apply it, and I believe we all came out as better leaders and stronger Christ followers because of it.

It's amazing how many answers are in the Bible to the great big questions of life. Every answer to every question lies within the Word of God. Over the two thousand years since Christ physically walked the earth, we've done a pretty good job of rearranging, complicating, and misinterpreting His words. In the early DC ("during Christ") days, He addressed mostly ordinary, uneducated, everyday type of people. He spoke to them in ways they could understand, such as using parables, which would help them "catch" the gospel. Jesus made it simple.

During the past couple of years, I've found myself returning to many of the simple Bible verses I tried so hard to memorize back in Sunday school. Some of those basic scriptures are the most life-changing and profound statements in the Word of God. And I've noticed a unique word that keeps popping up in many of those verses: *righteousness*. It's sort of like when you buy a car and then once you drive it off the lot, it seems like every third car you pass is *your* make and model. That's how the word *righteousness* has been for me lately. I've seen it show up all over the place—New Testament, Old Testament, in the words of Abraham, David, Jesus, Paul, and many other biblical writers and speakers. That word is everywhere in Scripture. I want to focus on two particular verses, featuring thoughts from my two favorite Bible heroes, Jesus and David.

Psalm 37:23: "The steps of a good man are ordered by the LORD" (NKJV). A few years ago, I was having a conversation with a drummer friend of mine, Phil, about how we make the big decisions in life—about jobs, relationships, significant moves, and so on. Phil brought up this verse and said something I've never forgotten. He said that if we can just focus on righteousness, and living right before God, then God would take care of everything else. Our steps would be ordered.

Our decisions, fears, and problems would all fall in line with God's path. And when God orders our path, He won't let us trip up. That's pretty freeing.

Matthew 6:33: "Seek first his kingdom and his righteousness, and all these things will be given to you." In this verse, Jesus was addressing something that we all deal with—worry. He was telling people, "Don't worry. God didn't make you to be anxious. He made you to be righteous." If you seek Him and His righteousness, then everything else will make sense. Everything else will be all right. The only way we receive righteousness is by faith in Christ. Not by what we do! It was Abraham's *belief* in God that made him righteous (Rom. 4:3). Because of Jesus, we are made righteous. It's amazing! Quit worrying about everything, and just seek His kingdom and His righteousness. Live like you were made to live—as the redeemed sons and daughters of the most high God.

So why am I saying all this stuff about righteousness in a book about leading worship with authenticity? Because you can't live and lead authentically if you aren't seeking first His kingdom, and His righteousness. All of our worship services, rehearsals, songwriting, playing instruments, and singing … all that stuff is included in "all these things." A year ago, I was talking to our teams at our first worship summit. Out of every topic I could've chosen, I spoke on righteousness. I believe that if we can grab the Matthew 6:33 concept, then everything else will be a byproduct of our righteous pursuit of God. When we seek Him and walk in righteousness, then we understand the need to be good stewards of our gifts, to play with excellence, to lead from a place of authenticity. According to Psalm 37, all the steps we take as worshippers, worship teams, and worship leaders will be prepared by God as we walk in righteousness. So be encouraged and fix your eyes on Jesus, because when you do that, everything else will fall into place.

There are countless other simple verses that pack a punch, and I could go on for days (or chapters) attempting to unwrap some of these amazing truths. But it will be much more authentic and more life changing if *you* dive into the Bible for yourself. The Holy Spirit is our modern-day interpreter of scriptures that were written many centuries ago. It's through the Spirit that we can read the Bible and find amazing application to our lives today.

The apostle Paul knew precisely what he was doing when he likened God's Word to a sword. The sword was one of the main weapons used in battle in the Roman Empire that Paul was living in. And if we lead worship without a knowledge and passion for God's Word, it's like going into war without a weapon.

A few years back, I went through a Bible-reading plan called "From Garden to City" with my church. We read through God's Word in a year, and it was the catalyst for me prioritizing an understanding of the Bible in my life. If you're not consistently getting into the Scriptures, then you're starving your spirit. In a world desperate for authenticity, it doesn't get any better than the Word of God. It's truth. It's where an authentic life of worship starts.

KNOW HIS VOICE

My kids could watch any movie that has penguins in it. Norah loves those little tuxedoed creatures. In fact, when Moses was born, my wife and I bought a stuffed penguin as a special gift for Norah to give to her baby brother. She still takes that little penguin to bed most nights, nearly a year later. One of the coolest things I've picked up from the many penguin flicks I've endured (I mean *enjoyed*) is how a baby penguin can recognize its specific parents' song. There can be a thousand penguins singing in the cold Arctic wind, and somehow a baby penguin can always pick out the particular sound of its parent's voice. How readily do we recognize God's voice as He calls out to us? It always breaks my heart when I hear worship leaders who have walked with the Lord most of their lives tell me they've never heard God speak. I respond with a simple question: "Are you listening?" He's always speaking, calling out to us, but too often we have so much chaos and busyness in our lives that we are unable to hear the soft, still whisper of His Spirit (1 Kings 19:12). A sound check is pointless if there's no one tuned in, listening to make sure the levels are set right. *We have become a culture that is great at hearing but awful at listening.*

One of my worship mentors, Danny Chambers, used to tell me all the time, "Spirit travels on sound." We can hear God's Holy Spirit whisper to us through the intimacy of musical worship. Likewise, we can also be the vessels of His voice as we let sound from our lips, filtered through His Spirit, transform lives here on earth.

God used prophets all throughout the Bible to speak His message to people. I love what Isaiah 51:16 says, "I have put my words in your mouth" (ESV). God is still putting His words into the mouths of those who would be used by Him. I grew up constantly hearing the phrase "Be His mouthpiece" in times of worship. And I believe worship leaders have a unique calling to prophesy His truth through powerful songs. We all know the power of words. We know they can carry life or death in them. James 3:9–10 shows us that our words and our sound can be used for the utmost good or evil: "With the tongue we praise our Lord and Father, and with it we curse human beings, who have been made in God's likeness. Out of the same mouth come praise and cursing."

If we want to be used as God's instruments in this world, we need to know His sound. If we aren't careful to take moments in our quiet times and actually *be quiet*, then we'll have a hard time hearing His voice. This is crucial in our corporate times of worship as well. One of the biggest "leap of faith" moments I've ever had in a service was in the middle of a worship set. We just stopped playing and allowed for a few moments of silence, for the congregation to tune in to God's whisper. It felt like an hour but probably didn't last more than thirty seconds. It was amazing to hear some of our church members speak about that after service, telling how it affected their idea of worship. Lean on God and trust in Him in those powerful moments when He needs to speak. *His voice is more important than yours.*

Many worship teams use in-ear monitors, and if you're familiar, then you've probably used a personal monitor mix box. So during a sound check, a vital necessity is setting up your own mix so that you can accurately hear what you're playing. If you can't hear the band, the vocals, and especially whatever instrument you are playing, trust me, it won't sound good out in the house. Every now and then when a singer on the team is yelling and not making a "joyful noise to the Lord," I'll go over to the monitor and check to see where the levels are set. Most times, the person is yelling to compensate for not hearing his or her voice at a normal singing level. Once the level is adjusted, the individual sings at a comfortable volume, and all is well in Worship Land.

Robert Sy is one of the most talented electric guitarists I know, and he can play pretty much any '80s solo in the book. But when he first auditioned for the NCC worship team, he had never used in-ear monitors before, so most of the audition was pretty rough. He kept apologizing for messing up, and thankfully, we gave him a second chance. Rob went home and got accustomed to in-ear monitors, came back after a couple of weeks, and rocked every guitar line. We still laugh about that first audition every time we get to play together. His audition was definitely not the true representation of how amazing he is on guitar.

We need to make sure we're hearing the right parts and muting the voices that aren't bringing life. We need to tune in to God's voice and tune out the chaos that so often distracts us from living devoted lives. When we hear His voice, we'll know how to speak, and sing, His truth.

FOR GROUP DISCUSSION OR PERSONAL REFLECTION

1. What does God's presence mean to you? Share, or reflect on, a time when you felt an undeniable connection to His presence.

2. Describe what a "Spirit-led" worship experience is.

3. What can you put in your daily life to make God's Word a priority?

4

CHECK YOUR ATTITUDE

I've chatted with and befriended dozens, maybe hundreds, of worship leaders over my last fifteen years in ministry. One thing I consistently hear in my conversations with other worship leaders is that a disconnect exists in their relationship with their lead pastor. Many worship leaders have been in situations where they experience constant fear that their pastor is disapproving and always second-guessing their leadership. I know I've battled not having the complete approval and affirmation of a pastor or two throughout the years. I also am willing to admit that I've had moments when I thought my ideas were way better than those of the lead pastor.

Whatever struggles you may have with your leadership, you have to realize that they *are* your leaders and God has placed you in *that* situation with *that* leader because He believes it's the right combination. I love the saying "Wherever you are, that's where God has you!"

He doesn't make mistakes, and He doesn't put us in the wrong places with the wrong people.

As worship leaders, we need to have the ability to *be led* as much as having the ability to *lead others*. We all must submit to our lead pastors' leadership, just as the lead pastors are submitting to Christ's leadership.

I'm incredibly grateful to serve under the leadership at National Community Church. I get to carry out the unique vision for worship that God has placed in my heart, but always in tandem with the overall vision at NCC. We have a group of core values that our worship team always falls in line with. One of the most disarming questions Pastor Mark first asked me in my initial job interview was "How can NCC play a part in what God has called *you* to?" Most of my interactions with other leaders have been the exact opposite: "How can you play a part in what *we* are doing?" I knew in that moment in my interview that NCC was a church I wanted to be a part of and that Pastor Mark was a leader I wanted to follow.

These days, I have a monthly touch point with Pastor Mark. We chat about what's going right and what needs to change. We celebrate victories and discuss growth opportunities. He challenges me to be a better leader, and according to him, I challenge him to be a better worshipper. I love what Proverbs 27:17 says: "As iron sharpens iron, so one person sharpens another." However, so many times we are tempted to regard the lead pastor as a higher-up who wants to dull our gifts instead of sharpen them. We need to realize that we work together! I know that the pastors at NCC and our worship leaders are all on the same side, and we actually have the same goal for worship every weekend—to see people encounter the presence of God.

KNOW YOUR WORTH

One way the enemy can distort our perception is when our hunger for affirmation goes unfed. Sometimes, there are weeks that go by when I don't have the chance to meet with my pastor, and I can quickly start to question my role and my worth. I start to think, *Why didn't he come up and say how awesome worship was this morning? Why didn't I get a text telling me how great the new song we wrote went over?*

We always assume the worst, don't we? At our last City Fathers Conference, I heard Dr. David Anderson, a pastor from Baltimore, use the phrase "Distance demonizes." You see, we always fill the gaps of time and space with the worst thoughts—about others and about ourselves—instead of assuming the best. Insecurity settles in, and we allow the lies of the enemy to be the loudest voice in the room and in our heads. I've seen countless worship leaders, myself at the top of the list, struggle with identity crisis. In those moments of questioning my worth, my wife reminds me, "Babe, if our pastor didn't believe in you, he wouldn't have you as the worship leader."

Self-doubt sucks. Seriously, it can suck the life right out of you. There were many years when I found my identity in my gift rather than in the Giver, and consequently, I had to fight through those years of seeking endless affirmation. The fact is, I had it all along. I love what my worship brother Chris Kim told me during a coffee meeting we had a while back: "We lead *from* acceptance, not *for* acceptance."

Earlier I wrote about Steph Hasler, my worship director predecessor. Steph is a great worship leader and vocalist, and in 2006, she experienced a time when all of her life's aspirations to be a singer were put to the test. Everything she had wrapped her identity and dreams in would change in a matter of minutes. She went in to see a doctor after feeling a lump in her throat. The medical staff did a biopsy, and the results revealed a tumor in her throat. Unsure of whether it was cancerous, the doctor told Steph she'd have to undergo surgery, during which her vocal cords would most likely be severed. The doctor knew she was a singer and added the devastating prognosis, "Don't plan on singing ever again."

The months that followed were filled with grief, anger, confusion, and doubt. She couldn't understand why God would give her a gift, one that she used to praise Him, only to take it away. Steph realized through this crisis that God was calling her identity to the surface. She needed to find her self-worth in Christ alone and not in what she could do or couldn't do. Through the experience, she realized that her voice was not *who* she was. It was an asset to her as a worship leader, but it wasn't *why* she worshipped.

Thankfully, after a second opinion from a different doctor, she was told the surgery could be done without severing her vocal cords. She could continue singing and leading worship. That surgery was a success, and since then she's been able to record several albums. She continues to wow audiences on both sides of the Atlantic Ocean with her voice.

Much like Steph, I've had to learn that my worth isn't in what I do or any gift that I carry. I know that if I always look for words of affirmation from people, I'll never have enough. However, I'll never feel empty if I can find my strength and worth in the Lord and in who He says I am.

I recently had lunch with Jordan Kauflin, a worship leader at Redeemer Church in Arlington, Virginia. We were talking about finding worth in who God says we are above anything our peers can tell us. Jordan said he found some amazing comfort in what David writes in Psalm 139. It's a psalm telling us that God formed us and knows our every move and our innermost thoughts and that He still loves us. Jordan put it this way: "We are fully known and deeply loved."

Nothing surprises God. He knows our deepest fears and our darkest thoughts, and yet He still fights for us, chases after us, and loves us as only a perfect Father could. The search for approval is over! False realities are exhausting. We can't live and lead authentic lives of worship until we step into the role that God has given us. And we will find that only if we know who He says we are.

KNOW YOUR ROLE

Get on the same page as your pastors. Don't seek affirmation from them, but find it in God. That will allow you to serve your church in the best way. Look for ways to honor your pastors, and always lead from humility. If there's a problem, deal with it. Don't let it simmer. I often find that worship leaders and pastors are under the biggest attack from Satan. They're also under the biggest microscope. That's because the worship leader and lead pastor are the ones in front of the congregation, and on the platform, every weekend. They are the two most visible roles in 99 percent of churches.

We carry targets on our backs, don't we? If the enemy can take out a pastor or a worship leader, then he has a chance to take out

the church. We can't afford an ounce of division in our relationships with our pastors.

At the end of the day, if we can't be led, we can't be used.
Earlier I talked about our team motto being "Only Servants" this
year, rooted in 1 Corinthians 4:1. The term "servant" refers to the
under-rowers in the hull of a ship. Think about if those oarsmen
didn't take leadership from their captain and everyone just rowed
in whatever direction and at whatever pace they felt like. The ship
would go in circles! It's much like if a band of musicians were
all playing off whatever chord chart they felt like bringing to a
rehearsal—the result would be awful. But when we allow ourselves
to be led, and we all work for the same goal, the ship can move and
the music will be a "sweet sound" to God's ear. Think of your lead
pastor as a captain and Jesus as the general. Never forget that the
church is not your audience but His bride!

The apostle Peter referred to leaders as shepherds and Christ as
the Chief Shepherd. He says, "Shepherd the flock of God that is
among you, exercising oversight, not under compulsion, but will-
ingly, as God would have you; not for shameful gain, but eagerly;
not domineering over those in your charge, but being examples to
the flock. And when the chief Shepherd appears, you will receive
the unfading crown of glory. Likewise, you who are younger, be
subject to the elders. Clothe yourselves, all of you, with humility
toward one another, for 'God opposes the proud but gives grace to
the humble'" (1 Pet. 5:2–5 ESV).

Peter ends his encouragement with the charge to live with humility. Godly leadership is never demanding, but always humble. If you
humble yourself to be led, you will in turn lead others with humility.

FOR GROUP DISCUSSION OR PERSONAL REFLECTION

1. How would you characterize the relationship you have with your lead pastor?

2. What verse of Scripture do you need to meditate on to find your affirmation in who God says you are?

3. Is there a friendship or relationship in your life that you would say helps keep your "humble meter" full?

5

CHECK YOUR GRATITUDE

What do you see when you close your eyes in worship? Maybe you just see the back of your eyelids and focus on the void. Or maybe you don't. When I close my eyes in worship and reflect on the lyrics of a song—whether it's about repentance, God's love, or His power—I always see pictures of God's faithfulness in my life. And that drops me to my knees. I don't deserve God's goodness. None of us do. The fact that He sacrificed His Son for us should make us bow down in eternal gratitude.

As worship leaders, we can take our cue from the apostle Paul, who said, "Let the word of Christ dwell in you richly, teaching and admonishing one another in all wisdom, singing psalms and hymns and spiritual songs, with thankfulness in your hearts to God" (Col. 3:16 ESV). God's goodness is way bigger than any song I could ever sing to Him. Yet I've found that when I sing in worship, it's a lot easier to express a heart of thanks. It's like that Stevie Wonder song

"I Just Called to Say I Love You." Music helps us express who we are to God.

When I think about the incredible faithfulness God has shown in my life, throughout my days on this earth, I can't help but respond in worship. There were times as a kid when I almost died, including nearly drowning at two years of age. And as a teenager, I got into some really bad car accidents. I see moments of answered prayers when I look at my wife and children. And if I'm ever leading worship when they are in the congregation, I usually get a little teary eyed catching a glimpse of my wife worshipping, one arm raised, the other holding on to Norah, while Moses is strapped on her chest. Can someone say "Supermom"? So when I close my eyes, I see all of these amazing pictures of life and much more. God's faithfulness leads me to gratitude. And gratitude leads me to worship.

Psalm 100 is described as a psalm for giving grateful praise. It says in verse 4, "Enter his gates with thanksgiving and his courts with praise." I used to read this verse and think that thanksgiving was something you did once you got *into* God's presence. However, after really diving into more and more scriptures about giving thanks, I believe Psalm 100 is saying it's actually a heart of gratitude that cata-pults us into God's presence. When we lead with thanksgiving, God opens the doors to His heart.

THE POWER OF THANKSGIVING

Giving thanks can also open the doors to God's power. We can see Jesus giving thanks in different circumstances, all throughout the

Gospels to show gratitude to His Father. Before feeding the five thousand in Matthew 14, Jesus gave thanks. Even during what was probably one of the scariest nights of His life, at the Last Supper, He gave thanks. Through Jesus we see that gratitude paves the way for miracles. By giving God thanks, we are blessing Him. That's one of the reasons we call prayer before a meal the "blessing." We bless the Lord when we thank Him, and as we saw in Deuteronomy 10, blessing the Lord is a major part of worship and a vital piece of leading worship.

Psalm 100 has really been a challenge to me, because there are so many things in this life that I take for granted. Growing up, I was blessed and fortunate enough to never go hungry. My mom didn't just heat up hot dogs and mac 'n' cheese—she usually went all out for just an average weekday dinner. What's more, every year on our birthdays, our parents would give us the option of going to our favorite restaurant or having Mom cook our favorite meal … and nine times out of ten, we'd pick Mom's home-cooked meal. It wasn't until my first semester in college that I realized just how good I had had it at home. Mom's cooking beat out a college meal plan any day. Whenever I'd go home for winter break, I made sure she knew just how much I appreciated her home cooking. Every now and then, my gratitude would even score me a few extra Ziploc bags full of leftovers to take back to school after break.

Having grateful hearts unlocks the doors not only in our worship but also in prayer. As Paul encourages us, "Do not be anxious about anything, but in every situation, by prayer and petition, with thanksgiving, present your requests to God" (Phil. 4:6). When we come to God with thanksgiving, instead of just our problems, it moves God to lean in and listen closer. Our prayer life shouldn't just consist of us nagging God when something doesn't go right. It should be full of us thanking Him for all the things that He's done and for the amazing love that He's shown us.

As a dad, I always love to hear my daughter say thank you. In fact, Norah has gotten so good at saying it that every now and then she says thanks before even asking for anything, just to build up her gratitude bank. She tried this trick on me not too long ago when she wanted dessert for breakfast.

Our morning routine usually involves her waking up at least two hours before the sun rises. She'll play with her dolls, sing a few songs, and dance to the latest VeggieTales or Disney soundtrack before coming to stun me awake with a shouted "Daddy!" two inches from my face. Then we'll head downstairs, and I'll change the diaper, get her a cup of juice, and then either Play-Doh-mashing or Cheerio-tossing activities ensue.

One particular morning, we went downstairs together, and she just started whining nonstop about wanting a popsicle. She preempted it with a "Fanks, Daddy. I wanna popsicle." She threw the thank-you in there with her cute little doe eyes and curly brown hair. It was a pretty good performance.

I said, "Norah, you can't have a popsicle. It's time for breakfast."

Thinking more insistence and volume might sway me, she said, "But, Daddy, I want a *popsicle!*"

I told her with slightly more edgy kindness in my tone, "Norah, you can have juice, but no popsicle."

Next, she decided to up the ante: "But, Daddy, I just want *two* popsicles!"

I wasn't sure how we got from one to two, but it was pretty hilarious at the time. Of course, I ended up giving her a popsicle, but at least it wasn't until after breakfast. You know, because she said thanks, or "fanks." I know, I'm a pushover.

By giving thanks, our eyes are opened to more of God's character and His order. We should always lead with thanksgiving. In fact, for a season of my life, I made it a discipline that the first words out of my mouth every morning when I got out of bed were "Praise the Lord" or "Thank You, God, for a beautiful day." I made a routine of giving thanks to God until it became habit.

We all have something to be thankful for, and that leads us to all sing a unique song in our worship times. When I sing the hymn "Great Is Thy Faithfulness," it means something totally different from when you sing it. That's because God's faithfulness to me is a unique story, just as His faithfulness in your life is unique to you. So when we gather every weekend worldwide as the worshipping church, God is hearing millions and millions of unique songs of praise. We may sing the same lyrics, but they represent different experiences. One of the coolest things about leading worship is recognizing that you have so many people coming in with different life experiences, different challenges, and different circumstances, and that worship is their chance to give it all to God. Everyone has a personal song of thanksgiving they can bring to Jesus in worship. Even when you find yourself in the rough seas of life, challenge yourself to find something to be grateful for, even if it's just the breath in your lungs. We should never let our current circumstance dictate how we worship God, because He is *always* worthy of our praise.

The very last verse in the very last psalm says, "Let everything that has breath praise the LORD" (150:6). So check your pulse. If you don't feel one, you need to call a doctor right away. But if you feel a pulse in your veins, then you have a beat in your heart, which means you have a song of praise to sing!

THANKFULNESS IN ACTION

One authentic way to show thanksgiving is by discipling others. When we take what we've learned and pour it out in others, it shows that we're not hoarding the knowledge and direction that the Lord has revealed to us. Every leader needs a mentor, and in turn we need someone to invest in. We're all called to be disciples and to make disciples. An important part of discipleship is learning from those who have gone before us and pouring into those who are coming after us.

Who on your worship team could you be pouring into? Moses had Joshua, Paul had Timothy, and Jesus had the twelve disciples. Whether you find an apprentice who is a potential worship leader, or a musician who needs some love, or someone from the youth group you know could use extra guidance, you'll never go wrong by giving your life away.

One of my favorite things about the ministry of NCC is our protégé program. Every year, we invite a group of young Christ followers to come and be a part of our team by walking alongside and doing life with our ministry leaders in our different departments. Our protégés come and plug in for yearlong discipleship, unpaid. It's an incredible display of faith, and each year I am challenged in my walk with Christ in new ways. We've had quite a few protégés in our worship department over the years, and I love having young worship leaders to invest in. I have a dream to one day be a part of starting a school of worship. What a privilege it would be to see many young, aspiring worship leaders grow in their understanding and calling to lead people in authentic worship.

The tough thing about being a mentor is recognizing that your disciples see you in every situation—the highs, the lows, when worship sets go great, and when they crash. Having a protégé is the constant reminder that you can't fake a life of worship. If you are wondering what the discipleship process looks like with our protégés, we've got a simple philosophy that guides the journey. It goes:

> Watch me as I do it.
> Let's do it together.
> I'll watch you as you do it.

Each of these steps is followed up with evaluation. Whether it's leading a worship set of songs, planning a project, or writing a song, it's a great way to do discipleship.

On the flip side of having someone to pour into, we also need someone we can constantly be learning from. I have several people in my life I can count on to be there in any sticky situation and to always hold me accountable for my actions. My parents have always been there to challenge me and encourage me when needed. However, we all know that the reason so many horrible singers go on *American Idol* is because Mom and Dad didn't have the heart to tell them how bad they really were. That's why we also need people outside our family who can speak into our lives with truth and grace.

Pastor Danny Chambers was one of those guys who looked beyond my "rock star wannabe" persona and called out the heart of David that was lying dormant in my life. He took me under his wing for a season and brought back a passion in me for worship and for the church when I was chasing after the things of the world. Not a bad guy to learn from, considering I grew up singing many of his songs in the church I went to as a kid. My drive for excellence in worship and my zeal for God's presence were largely fueled through mentoring and coffee hangouts with Pastor Danny.

Dave Schmidgall is another huge voice in my life. Dave is a dude who just calls it like he sees it. And trust me, he doesn't know how to call it any other way. He has known me since the first weekend I showed up in DC. He has my permission to call me out if he sees anything in my life that doesn't match up with the way a Christ-following leader should be living. He's also one of the few guys I can trust to challenge me to never settle for second best. If he senses I'm getting close to my comfort zone, or cruising in autopilot, he'll email or text to see if we can "hang." I'm grateful for those who challenge me to stretch myself and get out of my comfort zone. *People will often settle for mediocrity unless someone is pushing them toward greatness.*

Another mentor in my life is Pastor Heather Zempel, who challenges me by the way she leads. She's often told me "leaders are readers," so I rarely let a year slip by without finding at least a few books that challenge my spiritual walk and strengthen my faith. If you want to grow as a worship leader, don't just read books on worship. Surprisingly, the books that have had the most impact on my leadership and the way I lead worship have little to do with music. The more we learn and study—by reading books and blogs, watching podcasts, listening to albums, watching DVDs, taking notes during sermons, and diving into the Bible—the more ammo we'll have when we hit the battlefield of life and leadership.

You see, the moment we think we have things figured out is usually the same moment when God will prove to us that we don't. When we all realize that we're in endless process and that the journey of worship doesn't have a finish line on this side of eternity, we won't be satisfied with who we are or where we are. We will always have something else to learn and someone else to learn from. Don't be afraid to hang around those who are better than you are! That's one huge way I've grown in my musical ability—by placing far better musicians on the stage with me. Much like in a gym, you wouldn't hire a trainer who is scrawny and can lift less weight than you can. You want to be pushed and challenged by people who know what they're doing and can bring out the best in you!

FOR GROUP DISCUSSION OR PERSONAL REFLECTION

1. How are you making thanksgiving a part of your worship life?

2. What are three ways you can show your team appreciation and gratitude in the next couple of months? How can you make those actions part of your rhythm?

3. Identify one or two people in your life whom you feel God is calling you to mentor or disciple?

6

CHECK YOUR SAUCE

My drive to discover authentic worship hit warp speed last year, as our church's worship leaders drilled down to put together what our mission, vision, and values were as a team. Our values actually spell out an acronym: SAUCE, which stands for service, authenticity, unity, creativity, and excellence. It's a bonus that as musicians, we often used the phrase "bring the sauce" to mean "play your very best." Now it just has an extra kick whenever we say it in worship.

These five guiding values help shape every decision we make as a team. I also think it would be hard to lead worship in a way that invites and honors God's presence without these values.

As I mentioned in the last chapter, my mom is an incredible cook. I'm forever grateful that she's passed on much of her cooking and baking knowledge to my wife. It's a sheer miracle that I don't weigh five hundred pounds. Mom has several cookbooks out in stores nationwide, and she's won her fair share of food contests.

She'll tell you that in everything she cooks, it just takes the right ingredients. If you have too much or too little of something, or if the right ingredient is missing, it can spoil the whole dish. Now I want to dive into the SAUCE values and explore how these ingredients work together to make a pretty mean worship sauce. And much like my face after I eat a plate of spaghetti, I hope this sauce sticks with you.

SERVICE

I told you that one of our vision themes was "Only Servants," so I don't need to dive too heavily into this ingredient. Service needs to be in every worship leader's core values, because if we aren't serving our churches, we're probably thinking only of ourselves.

My good friend and mentor Simon Dixon likens worship leaders to waiters. He says good waiters or hosts will serve you without drawing attention to themselves. It takes skill, maturity, and humility. Now, I should tell you that Simon is from England, where he served alongside Tim Hughes at Holy Trinity Brompton. Being English means he has one of those awesome accents, so everything he says counts twice. That's one of the many reasons I love having coffee or lunch with him. We must remember we're called to serve others. It's okay for us all to aspire to greatness, but greatness probably doesn't look as flashy as the world around us has made it out to be. In fact, Jesus tells His disciples these powerful words in Matthew 23: "The greatest among you shall be your servant. For those who exalt themselves will be humbled, and those who humble themselves will be exalted" (vv. 11–12 ESV). The amazing thing is that when we actually take the low road and place others' lives ahead of our own, we become great in our Father's eyes. God exalts those who walk in humility, and when He exalts us, it's a beautiful thing.

Jesus was the most authentic example of humility this world has ever seen. Even as the very Son of God, He didn't come expecting everyone to bow down and honor Him. He came to us not with pomp and circumstance, but born in the most humble of ways. Matthew 20:28 says that Christ "did not come to be served, but to serve." If we want to live a life that reflects Jesus, we need to live as servants.

AUTHENTICITY

This whole world is looking for the real deal, but we certainly have plenty of the opposite. We have an epidemic of fakeness in our generation, and we've allowed ourselves to muddy the lines so much that we sometimes struggle to identify what is true and what is false.

One reason stripped-down, acoustic-sounding bands have blown up on the pop-culture music scene over the past few years is that people sense authenticity. Bands such as Mumford and Sons, Bon Iver, and The Lumineers have found their way from back-alley coffeehouses to center stage at the Grammys because people know there's nothing fake about their music. They sound the same in a living room as they do in a music venue filled with thousands of people and a state-of-the-art light show. Authenticity basically translates into "being real."

We recently had a team night where different members of our team shared their testimonies. They shared about personal battles, heartbreak, and loss. They were open and vulnerable. You can't have authenticity without vulnerability. People will always spot a fake, and vulnerability removes the masks, takes down the guard, and lets the world see who we really are, scars and all. *Your scars may be someone else's healing.*

Joel Buckner is a close friend and one of the most anointed worship leaders I know. At this particular team night, he shared about his past, being abused at a young age, and how for years when he led worship, it was out of pain. He eventually allowed God to be his healer and completely restore his life, and now Joel leads out of a place of victory every week at NCC's Lincoln Theatre location. Right after JB shared this with our team, he went into a song of worship that spoke of God's grace and redemption. When we sang that together as a team, there wasn't a dry eye in the house. That's not emotion; that's authenticity.

Let me bring it a little closer to home for me. When I was a sophomore in college, I was leading worship at the largest campus ministry at Virginia Tech every week. Life was pretty sweet, and being in that place of influence earned me a lot of friends and opportunities. However, being in the spotlight also brings a lot more eyes on every move you make, and I learned this lesson the hard way. My girlfriend came over late one night after class to watch a movie, and when it was done, instead of walking across campus back to her dorm, she just crashed in my room. Even though nothing happened that night, we definitely gave the wrong appearance.

Somehow word got back to our leadership that my girlfriend had spent the night with me, and in a very public and humiliating way, I was taken out of the worship-leader role. My friends all of a sudden didn't want to hang out, and all of the opportunities to lead worship seemed to come to a drastic halt. It was a full six months before I gathered the strength to lead a worship song again, and thankfully God's grace taught me a ton of valuable lessons in my hiatus. In those months, I let God do a work in my life. I came out of it a better worship leader and closer to God's heart.

I often use the phrase "worship through hardship." It comes from the life of a willow tree. The resilient willow tree has roots that allow it to bend and bow in a storm, but not break. It stands strong against the wind, as its roots go deep into the earth. When we worship through hardship, we stand strong in a storm. Our worship team even has a Facebook page by that name, and people across our different campuses post prayer requests that we all pray for and lift up to God as a worship family. And that's what happens when you get real with your teams and the people you do life with.

Community equals chemistry. Every band will tell you that what makes the music work is chemistry between the musicians. You can't manufacture it. You just have it—or you don't! When you care for the people on your team and the people in your church, you start to see community forming. And community offstage becomes chemistry onstage. Get out of the green room and into the church pews, or theater seats, or folding chairs—whatever seating your church has.

The apostle Paul tells us, "For our struggle is not against flesh and blood, but against the rulers, against the authorities, against the powers of this dark world and against the spiritual forces of evil in the heavenly realms" (Eph. 6:12). Worship is warfare, and just like any soldier would say, you want to know that the people you're going into battle with have your back. When we can be genuine with one another, share our struggles, and lift one another up in prayer, we are able to worship from a standpoint of being a band of brothers and sisters. We can do a lot more damage to the enemy as a unified front!

UNITY

Earlier I mentioned my involvement in a project that had several churches across the country coming together to write, record, and release original worship songs birthed in unity. The album released in August 2013 at the Assemblies of God General Council Conference. However, the vision started nearly a year prior, in October 2012, when three of those churches came together in Dallas to write songs for the album.

Let me tell you, the Holy Spirit's presence in that room was so tangible that we could sense something special at work. The psalm came to life: "How good and pleasant it is when God's people [brothers and sisters] live together in unity!" (133:1 ESV). There were no puffed-up egos or stuck-up attitudes—just unity in the presence of God. From that first meeting of the minds, several songs came about that I believe shaped the entire album. This project was the catalyst in my life for a passion to see God's church united, and working together as one, for the same team.

There are many spheres where unity needs to be developed for our churches to be effective. First, we must have unity within our own church body. Most of us know Abraham Lincoln's famous phrase "A house divided against itself cannot stand." But actually the great president took his cue from Jesus, who was quoted as saying the same words in Mark 3:25. Is your worship team united, is your church staff united, and finally, is your congregation united? As leaders, we're first and foremost called to our own house. In this day and age, so many ministry leaders get eyes bigger than their calling. We start to think of how we can make an impact on the world at large and write songs that will influence the global church, all the while neglecting the very people in front of us who were called to lead. I've heard many say that a pastor's first church is his or her own family. If you don't lead your family well, your church will soon be in disarray. Most of us know firsthand someone, or some church, where this has become a reality.

I started a small group for the worship leaders at NCC, and ever since, our leaders have been unified in a powerful way, knowing that when we step foot on a Sunday morning stage, we are joining our brothers and sisters across multiple campuses. We even called the small group The Tribe, as it truly reflects a band of worship warriors.

The next area of our lives that we're called to bring unity to is our city. Sadly, many churches have an "us versus them" mentality, and there can often exist a spirit of backstabbing and gossip about other churches in our own backyard. God wants to see *collaboration* instead of *competition* when it comes to His church. I pray that in our churches we realize it's not about the name over the door, but it's about the name preached inside. So whose name do we care about more—our own or the name above every other name? If all I do is pump up the church that I'm a part of and close my eyes to God's worldwide church, then I'm missing the point.

So, in this spirit, I challenged our worship leaders to connect with other worship leaders in our city, and we had our first-ever

DC Worship Initiative breakfast in May 2013. Nearly forty worship leaders from around the city, from different churches, showed up to share, pray, and encourage one another. It was incredible, and the friendships forged from this unified gathering have had a huge impact on the way I see the body of Christ.

Another sphere we need to bring unity to is our world. We are all called to carry out the Great Commission (Matt. 28). If you've never been on an international missions trip, I would say put that on your to-do list. God has illuminated Himself during many moments on such trips I've been on, and these moments have broadened my life perspective and sharpened my purpose perspective.

I want to see God bless the church across town just as much as I want to see Him bless my home church. And if we all work together in accordance with the Holy Spirit, we can change our city, our nation, and eventually our world. It's not about us! The more we take the focus off ourselves and how awesome *our* ministry is, the more Christlike our ministry will become. *How many more lives would be reached for the gospel's sake if we didn't care who got the credit?* When we are intentional about building unity in the church, and in our teams, we become less concerned about ourselves.

A few years back, Pastor Mark Batterson felt the spiritual urge to see churches in DC come together and sit under the teaching of various local pastors who had been in ministry for fifteen years or more. It was a powerful day of honoring those who are paving the way for the next generation. This has formed into an annual event called City Fathers, and it's become one of my favorite days of the year. At the first ever City Fathers conference, Stuart McAlpine, who pastors Christ Our Shepherd Church in DC, made a powerful statement that I often reference when talking on unity to worship leaders. He said, "Our churches aren't meant to be separate wells, but rather an irrigation system for our city." We are meant to complement one another in ministry, not compete with one another.

Too often, especially on worship teams, we see people church hopping. The result is that churches end up trading Christians among themselves instead of reaching the world outside the four walls of the church building. Side note: One way we've tried to deter this in our worship team is by requiring everyone who comes to audition to have been in regular attendance at NCC for at least three months. That requirement would be a lot longer, but with a city as transient as DC, we have people with us for an average of only two years.

When we lead with humility, we default to unity. Ask yourself the question: "Am I leading the team or leading *with* the team?" Leading worship and doing ministry are not about us—they're about His kingdom, and His kingdom is one built in unity.

Mark 3:24 says, "If a kingdom is divided against itself, that kingdom cannot stand." Division kills. Unity builds. It gets a lot easier to take the focus off ourselves when we give leadership away. I love seeing our worship leaders rise to the occasion, and I'm constantly blown away by each of their unique ways of leading. It's not easy to trust others to lead, especially if you're used to seeing things done a certain way. But however things may get done, as long as they do get done, they're getting done.

We're all familiar with delegating responsibility, but that's task oriented, whereas giving leadership away is more purpose driven. Sadly, though, in the dog-eat-dog world that we live in, church leaders are often afraid to give people the opportunity to lead. Maybe we don't really know how to properly empower others. Maybe we feel like we are somehow passing off our role or not doing our job. Maybe it's a pride issue, as we are afraid someone else will do the job better than we do and we'll be replaced.

Here's the reality: You can't hold on to your job forever. You can either give it up intentionally or unwillingly. When you work yourself out of a job, in most cases it ensures you will always have one. Giving leadership away multiplies your influence and frees you to concentrate on what you do best. Don't just delegate when it's a necessity. Don't delegate as a means of damage control. Make it a habit, because it's an expression of discipleship. If you are stunting someone else's growth, it will result in your stunting your own growth. Growing people grow people. Look for the best in others, and call it out. Then you'll see them become the best leaders they can be. Great leaders come from great leaders who have invested in them.

One way that we've been able to give leadership away to those on our worship teams, outside of our staff, is by finding "champions." These are people who serve faithfully on our teams, consistently go above and beyond what's required, and take our "Only Servants" theme to the next level. We have both "community champions" and "instrument champions." At each of our campuses, one person is in charge of making sure we're fostering community within the team. That person puts together game nights, outings, after-church lunches, and other activities. Susan Manchester, the community champion at our Lincoln Theatre campus, has a "community contagiousness." She does a great job of not only putting together events for our team, but she also sends out a weekly recap email to keep us all in the loop on happenings, as well as prayer requests for those in our church. We also have the instrument champions, who take leading on their particular instrument seriously by challenging other musicians to continually grow and improve. They host clinics for other musicians to develop their skills. Clinics also give people an opportunity to meet other musicians who play the same instrument. We call Jack our mad scientist on the keyboards. He doesn't believe in doing things halfway. From his setup on Sundays to how he connects with all of our keys players, Jack goes all out—and all in. He also works for one of the three-lettered government agencies, so we're pretty sure his last name might be Bauer.

NCC Worship hosts Team Nights at the end of every month. Hillsong Church broke the mold with the way they do team nights, and we've taken a lot of pointers from them as well as many other churches. These nights have been epic in building community among our campuses. We kick off every team night with a meal, because let's be honest, who doesn't want a free dinner? Then we have a time of worship, followed by a short message. I love inviting worship leaders from other churches to share with our team. Will Herron and Chris Kim are a couple of worship leaders from other churches who both shared inspiring and profound messages with our team. Building relationships with worship leaders outside your home church will give you a bigger vision and greater love for your city.

Team night is our monthly way of building unity. In fact, if you break up the word *community*, you essentially get two words: *common* and *unity*. What we share in common can often be what unifies us. And in worship, we know that our common denominator is to see the name of Jesus lifted up in our praise. I highly encourage any leader reading this to create some form of team night within your culture.

You'll see authentic community rise up as a result, and people won't only feel "a part" of what you're doing; they'll also feel like shareholders.

CREATIVITY

"If you always do what you've always done, you'll always be what you've always been." That phrase was in a message I heard a pastor preach when I was twelve years old, and I've never forgotten it. Creativity doesn't just push us to invent brand-new things; it also prompts us to reinvent things that have been done a thousand times. Worshipping God is one of those things. However, because there are so many easy routes to travel in the sphere of worship, we often just set creativity aside because we don't have the time or capacity to create. This might be the case if you find yourself playing the same ten or fifteen songs in worship over a few months. It's one thing to go for consistency, but it's no excuse for coasting.

When you let your worship life hit cruise control, you operate in fear rather than faith. To be creative in worship takes faith, and that's where the fun part comes in. Sometimes you'll mess up, and that's okay. If you include "How Great Is Our God" (one of my all-time favorites) the same way every Sunday because you're afraid your team will mess up any song with more than four chords, you're not allowing the artistry of worship to come out. I saw Chris Tomlin in concert earlier this year, and he opened the night with that song. And he did it in a way I'd never heard before, with new instrumentation and layering the parts with his musicians coming into the song one by one. Creativity in action!

So how do we exercise creativity? If you aren't integrating rehearsals in your worship culture, then you might not be setting your teams up to grow their creative edge. Rehearsals are the place where creative ideas and transitions can be worked out and fine-tuned. Weekend services are the place where your homework can come to life. Know what you can do on stage and *kill* it. Know what you can't do and work on it.

In Exodus 35:30–33, we can see a call to creativity when Moses was outlining the work of the tabernacle: "Then Moses said to the Israelites, 'See, the LORD has chosen Bezalel son of Uri, the son of Hur, of the tribe of Judah, and he has filled him with the Spirit of God, with wisdom, with understanding, with knowledge and with all kinds of skills—to make artistic designs for work in gold, silver and bronze, to cut and set stones, to work in wood and to engage in all kinds of artistic crafts." I'd venture to say that Bezalel's anointing is the same kind of anointing we can experience in leading worship, when we also are filled with the Spirit. Creativity is wonderful, but when you add the Holy Spirit to the equation, you've got the double dose of inspiration.

We are created in the image of the mastermind of the universe. How could we *not* reflect that with the desire to create? As worship leaders, we get to work with one of the most creative mediums in the world—music. There's no end to what you can do with a song when it comes to instrumentation, style, lyrics, and dynamics. Music is an artist's pallet with an endless number of colors to paint with. Music is the universal language. *Music has a way of reaching someone's heart without ever asking for permission.* Music can find the rare cracks in a world crisscrossed by walls, both visible and invisible,

and realign our differences back to that unifying theme found in the
Scriptures—that we're all created in the image of God. And if music
speaks directly to the heart, worship is the act of giving your heart.
It ascribes worth to something and expresses it in one of the most
creative and expressive forms.

But just like everything in life, with creativity you can have too
much of a good thing. One of the hardest disciplines with creativity
is operating within limits. That's why I often say that *creativity is
"freedom within a framework."* I pray every day that my daughter
would learn this lesson. I love how active Norah is, and she would
live outside in our backyard if we had a backyard (the joys of city
living). One thing she loves to do is jump. She does her bunny hop
about thirteen hours out of a twenty-four-hour day. We're constantly
telling her, "Norah, don't jump on the couch." She is allowed to
jump on the ground or outside. Heck, if my wife's not around, I'll
even occasionally let her jump on her bed. But she's not allowed to
jump on the couch, because there's a pretty big drop-off from the
couch to the ground. Once a week, she learns the lesson the hard
way, as she'll jump on the couch and, sure enough, crash into the
windowsill or the couch arm or land on the floor. Rules exist not to
constrict us, but to free us. Rules exist to keep us safe, even when we
don't realize what safety is.

At one of our first-ever team nights, our Lincoln Theatre campus
pastor, Dave Schmidgall, shared about the blessing of limitations.
Being a huge jazz enthusiast, he explained to us how the beautiful
art of improvisation makes sense. In college, I took a couple of jazz
music survey courses and have high respect for some of the legends,
such as Charles Mingus, Dizzy Gillespie, and John Coltrane. I'm

not talking about Ron Burgundy playing the jazz flute here. There's a way that jazz artists seem to effortlessly play and make any standard chord progression stretch the limits of time and space. I always thought when I saw a jazz performance that all the solos were off the cuff, made up on the spot. But behind every note in improvisation are thousands of hours of practice, years of listening, and dozens of transcribed solos. Every flawless performance and ear-catching riff is backed by tons of private instruction and tough lessons picked up in jam sessions. There is indeed freedom within framework.

In 2 Corinthians 3, Paul says that where the Spirit of God is, there is freedom. Sometimes, you and your team will need to go off script and discern where the Holy Spirit is leading at that time. Maybe it's a musical interlude or repeating a phrase or singing to the Lord a new song. Spontaneous, improvisational worship can be a powerful and life-changing experience. But it doesn't happen by accident. It's the result of hard work on our part, coupled with trust in the Spirit's moving. Worship improvisation, or following the leading of the Spirit, is the crossroads of discipline and freedom. The greatest freedom comes out of constraints. Creativity is always best enjoyed and expressed within a proper framework; otherwise it is just chaos.

EXCELLENCE

In the realm of worship, there has always been the discussion about performance-driven worship versus Spirit-led worship. We've probably all been in that service (or maybe even led worship in that service) where it feels like the freeform jazz odyssey at the end of

Spinal Tap. You know, it's the one where you worship for an hour and a half just playing E, B, and A till your fingers feel like they're going to fall off.

I've also been on the other side, leading worship at a televised event, where the producer gave me a death stare if I went 3.5 seconds over the allotted time we were given for "Our God." Don't you dare sing that bridge again!

The truth is, we have all kinds of churches because the world has all kinds of people. If there was one expression of the church that had all the right methods, styles, and answers, then we would probably have only one church. When you can live in that tension of striving for a top-notch performance while yielding to whatever the Holy Spirit desires to do, you can find a beautiful balance and harmony in worship.

At the end of the day, most of us can agree that the Holy Spirit isn't limited by time and space. God can do what He needs to do, how He needs to do it. I've seen God's presence blow up the joint in a three-song, thirteen-minute set. And I've seen Him wreck a place over the course of three hours, with just one song being played (how those musicians didn't get bored can only be by God's grace).

When it comes to performance and presence, I don't think the two are mutually exclusive aspects of worship. As someone who has led worship at churches that identify with both sides, there are some nuggets an authentic leader can take from each background. Too often we overlook the need for excellence in an environment that has a high focus on the movement of the Holy Spirit. On the flip side, there are many churches that end up putting God in a box by never allowing the Holy Spirit to have His way, which might sometimes mean veering from the production run sheet every now and then.

I started to think of the word *performance* a little differently after Norah was born. She is a little princess who loves to dance and sing. Without fail, every time she sings a classic Disney song, or does her special dance, she says, "Daddy, watch!" And she'll continue saying that until she gets my attention. As soon as I start watching, I can tell her whole world lights up. The only thing she cares about is if I approve of her song and dance. You better believe I do! And nothing in this world makes me smile like those simple, precious moments. My little girl performing for her dad and no one else—it doesn't get any better than that.

Maybe you can see where I'm going with this. When we worship our King, it's a music recital in the heavenly realms. And He smiles with every ounce of love in His heart when He sees His kids singing and dancing just for Him. So maybe we need a renewal in the way we think about performance in worship. As long as it's not for the applause of man but to bring joy to our Father in heaven, it's a good thing.

With that being said, performance is a pretty common area of discussion in worship circles, and I think God spoke to me in a unique way on the topic. I had a dream not too long ago where I was leading worship in a massive arena. The setup included an epic band, full choir, high-tech light show, four-tiered stage, and thousands upon thousands of people out in the crowd (aka "congregation"). It was everything a performer could want. Suddenly, I started having a ton of technical difficulties with my wireless mic. I was trying to do this really grand entrance on a song, and the sound began to cut in and out, causing a ruckus on stage. A pastor friend of mine showed up at the side of the stage with a new microphone and called out, "Kurtis, use this one." And then another pastor friend slowly walked up next to me and whispered, "Kurtis, we're missing the point of worship right now."

I grabbed a working mic and spoke to the thousands of people in front of me, saying these words: "I'm afraid we've created such a visual spectacle that no one here wants to close their eyes in prayer, afraid that they'll miss out on something to see."

Then all of a sudden, my two-year-old crawled over my wife into our bed and woke me up with a knee to the back. So I quickly grabbed my phone and began to write down what I believe the Holy Spirit was speaking to my heart through that dream.

We are a sight-based culture. We love all things visual. Think of the hundreds of movies released every year, the fashion industry, and pretty much everything this world says is attractive—it's all centered on catching our eye.

I'm concerned that as Christ followers, we've neglected to keep ourselves from listening to 1 John 2:16, which says, "For everything in the world—the lust of the flesh, the lust of the eyes, and the pride of life—comes not from the Father but from the world." *We get so preoccupied with reaching our culture that we adapt to it rather than influence it.* In all of our attempts to reach people with the visual, let's not miss our calling to connect people to the spiritual. We can capture people's eyes and still completely miss their hearts.

As worship leaders, we face a very present danger of getting caught up in the visual world. We see the Instagram uploads every Sunday of churches across the globe with stunning stages and wonder why we are stuck with a couple of IKEA lamps and a PA system from the Dark Ages. I'm not at all saying there's anything wrong with a phenomenal light show, a killer sound system, or a cutting-edge stage design. I fully believe we are called to be the best, and that is one thing our culture *does* well. When we go all out to reach people for the kingdom and our motivation is to point people to Jesus, then we really can't go wrong (whether it's state of the art or stripped down to the bone). But at the core of our worship, we should remember Amos 5. The Old Testament prophet warns the people of the time that God wasn't interested in their festivals, songs, or offerings: "Away with the noise of your songs! I will not listen to the music of your harps" (v. 23). God was after their hearts, and He longed for a nation that would live in justice and righteousness.

Imagine Jesus showing up to a church service where you are leading worship. Would He feel like an exalted King, or would He feel like a concert attendee? Would He say, "Away with the noise of your songs"? Or would He welcome your praise as an offering to the Lamb of God? Let's be sure not to get so caught up chasing the look of excellence that we forget the heart of worship. Whether you've got a packed-out stadium ready to shout to God or a small group of people in a living room longing to cry out, remember that you lead people, not experiences.

Over the past decade, *excellence* is one of those words that has gotten a bad wrap, because so often we confuse it with *perfection*. Jad Gilles, from Hillsong Worship, once said in a Q&A forum, "Excellence isn't perfection. Excellence is our very best." My foundation for leading worship always starts with the philosophy of "Excellence meets Simplicity."

The skill of leading worship is not about how impressively we play, but about how we can play less and give space for the Lord to move in worship. It goes without saying that we should always seek to play skillfully, as David did, and give our very best out of deep gratitude to Jesus, who gave everything that we might live resurrected and grace-filled lives. He held nothing back from us, so how could we hold anything back from Him? Genuine worship leaders know that you don't pursue excellence in music just to sound like a well-oiled machine. You do it because the God of the universe, and King above all, deserves nothing less.

I encourage you to practice regularly both alone and with your worship band. And know the difference between practice and rehearsal. Don't hold your team to a standard that you're not willing to live by yourself. I'm often convicted that I don't practice enough, and I let my need to run scales and other fundamentals fall by the wayside as I work on writing songs, finding cool synth and guitar tones, and engaging with other glamorous parts of music. We've heard that practice makes perfect, and I'll be the first to tell you that's not the case. I do, however, believe that practice paves the way for excellence.

One practical, yet often difficult, way to unify a team of musicians and worshippers is to allow for a culture of feedback. This shows that it's not only about the actual worship song leader and whatever skill set the person may have, but it's about the whole team coming together to create a beautiful sound of worship that leads people and honors God. The reason I know feedback breeds unity is because asking for someone's thoughts on a song takes humility, as it brings in the collective thought. It's something I have to be intentional about in every rehearsal. Naturally, I come into a rehearsal with certain parts, transitions, and songs all worked out. I produce albums throughout the year, so it's hard for me to sometimes take off that producer hat. But that's why I have to be intentional. I'm sure many of us listen to a certain song and want to perform it just like the album, which is always a starting point for me. That definitely necessitates practice.

I always say if the producer and worship band put all that time into making the recording good, we can take the time to learn the parts they put blood, sweat, and tears into. However, when we open ourselves to creativity and try new things, familiar songs can have a fresh edge. Nearly every time I've taken a moment to ask the team what their thoughts are on a song, we come out with something that is really fun, dynamic, and worshipful. It's creativity in motion. *When your team feels that what they bring to the table matters, they'll start to bring stuff to the table.*

Feedback in a sound check is a bad thing, but feedback within a worship team is great. We need to lead people to know their value, both in our teams and in our church congregations. If everyone is afraid to speak his or her mind, then feedback will never happen. Be intentional about asking your team what they think, and as people open up little by little, you'll be amazed to see how much more your team gets excited about rehearsals. They will be eager to fully participate in the creativity behind the worship offering you bring to God. Every great leader I've served under has been open to feedback. It's how we grow and get better at what we do. This doesn't mean we always put the suggestions into action, but it does mean we listen and value others' opinions and ideas with open minds and hearts.

Feedback also goes hand in hand with evaluation. This is a critical part to growing our worship teams and ourselves. You can't have excellence without evaluation. After most of the church services I lead, I quickly gather the team before tearing down and reflect briefly on the worship service. Musically, what did we do well and what do we need to work on? Spiritually, were we tuned in to what God was doing that morning or were we spacing out in our little zones? These are prime moments to share feedback and evaluate, because it's not only fresh on our minds, but there's a spirit of receptivity in the air that welcomes growth.

Now, I've jacked up enough times in the good ol' "compliment sandwich" method to know that sometimes you just have to be real with people and give it to them straight. I was once at a point with my team where every time they heard me compliment them, they braced themselves, knowing an uppercut was coming. You see, people will receive feedback only when there is relationship. If I trust someone, then I'll listen to what he or she has to say.

So here's what not to do: If you've never given feedback to your team, don't let your first feedback session come minutes after an incredible moment of Spirit-led worship. I wouldn't recommend going up to the guitarist and busting his chops for that one wrong note in the third song, even though it stood out like a sore thumb. Sometimes I've gone out of a worship set thinking that one wrong note ruined everything—only to have more people say God spoke to them in that particular service than in the dozens of perfectly executed worship sets. It's a great reminder that worship doesn't depend on us.

Be careful not to limit your feedback to only the negative things that need correction. Look for the good, and call it out. One of my drummer friends, Bryan, had the hardest time when we first started using click track in our worship sets. He was a great drummer, but for some reason, things just didn't click (sorry, I had to). There were quite a few weeks that we would rehearse with the click, but when it came time for service to start, we had to turn it off because he was fighting it so bad. But we stuck with it. After a couple of months, we started calling him the "Human Metronome" because he had become so solid with it. You better believe after his first service of conquering the click, I pulled him aside and affirmed him for going after it. He recently moved with his family to Pennsylvania and texted me that I had ruined him on the click, because he can now tell every time a band is playing without one. His timing is like a clock, and I don't think he'll ever *not* play with a click again. The positive feedback worked its magic. Feedback and evaluation are always taken best with a side of grace.

Might I even suggest that Jesus took feedback? In Mark 8, we read where Jesus and the disciples are on the road to a village, headed toward their next revival tent meeting. Jesus asks the famous question: "Who do men say that I am?" Reading this through the lens of a leader, I started to think that Jesus may have actually been doing more than asking a challenging question to His disciples to test their faith. He may have been soliciting feedback from His disciples. It's very possible that Jesus, having recently performed some high-profile miracles, was the talk of the town and was interested in what kind of gossip was circling around about Him. Not that it would faze Him, especially when the disciples answer by saying He's been likened to John the Baptist, Elijah, and other prophets. But Jesus valued what His disciples thought. He wanted to know where their hearts were and how they were processing the epic ministry they were living out. That's why Jesus further prompts Peter by asking, "Well, who do *you* say that I am?" Of course, Peter gives the right answer: "You are the Messiah."

Jesus always is doing something deeper than what appears on the surface. We could read this passage and just think that Jesus was making sure that His main dudes were still His main dudes. However, this was a pivotal moment—away from the crowds, on a stroll to the next village—that Jesus had a chance to build the unity of His team. He asked them an open-ended question, followed by a pointed one. He asked for feedback and then spoke truth into the matter.

You see, Jesus did everything in His ministry *with* the disciples. Part of having a great team is when everyone feels a part of the conversation. Everyone feels invited to the table. We know that Jesus invited His disciples not only to follow Him but also to be a *part* of His ministry. *They weren't his busboys—they were his waitstaff.* He loved His team and valued their thoughts. And that's one reason why they were willing to lay down their lives for Him.

If we want to be great worship leaders, we should listen to and be inspired by other worshippers who are leading their congregations in powerful experiences of God's presence. Not as copycats, but as students. I go to as many concerts as I can, both Christian and mainstream, to find inspiration and learn. Excellence matched with humility looks a lot like learning from others. Every year, we find at least one conference to attend together as a worship team, and each one of our staff members gets something different from those times. If we're not learning, then we're stagnant. And we can't run the road of excellence if we stay in the parking lot.

Another reason we ought to pursue quality as a worship team is for the sake of our congregations. A common prayer I have before I lead our church in worship is that God would help me "stay out of the way." We need to realize that any mistake on stage is a potential distraction off stage. For those in our church seats who may not have ever experienced the power of God's presence, let's do everything we can to usher them in without being a hindrance. In most church services I've been a part of, the music is the first thing that happens. That opening praise chorus sets the tone for the entire service. As worship leaders, we are setting the table for God to serve the main course. Are we setting it with the finest china or with plasticware?

The sidekick to excellence should always be simplicity. Whether you are at a church that has one gathering in one location or a multi-site church with dozens of services happening over a weekend, never lose sight of Jesus. Never lose the beautiful simplicity of the gospel. We all need to do things with excellence, whether you're a worship leader, a guest greeter, or a youth pastor. But if our passion for excellence gets in the way of our heart for people, we need to hit the brakes. May we never get so caught up in doing things *for Jesus* that we *miss Jesus*.

Earlier I spoke of my friend Joel Buckner and his vulnerability in sharing his testimony. Joel and I love to lead and write worship songs together. We serve alongside each other at NCC these days, and we were on the same worship team together in Nashville before we both moved to DC. We both began to feel a spirit of performance over a passion for God's presence in our circles of friends and in the churches where we were serving. It was then that we wrote a song called "Burn It All Down," which gospel artist Lexi later recorded. The second verse and chorus talk about how sometimes our lives need a course correction:

If my ambition blocks the path of where you lead
And if my drive directs my heart from destiny
Lord, if I ever lose my way, in my own desire
Overtake me with your holy fire

Burn it all down, and leave only you
I let nothing stand in the place of your truth
All that we've made, and buildings we've raised
All that's in vain, you can take it away, and leave only you

In all that we do for the sake of advancing the kingdom of God and the message of Jesus, may we never lose the beauty of a simple love for Jesus. Worship is, and will always be, a matter of the heart.

FOR GROUP DISCUSSION OR PERSONAL REFLECTION

1. Come up with a list of core values for your personal worship life, and for your team, if you lead one.

2. What can you put in your weekly rhythm to keep creativity alive in you and your team?

3. To build unity outside your church walls, reach out to three worship leaders at other churches in your area. Take them to coffee, and get to know one another!

7

CHECK YOUR PURPOSE

During one of our 2014 team nights, we had our discipleship pastor, Heather Zempel, come and share her heart. She has a knack for finding the hidden gems in Scripture that most of us would miss even if we read them a hundred times. The particular message she spoke that night was on the priests of Zadok from Ezekiel 44. When was the last time you read from the book of Ezekiel and had a worship team takeaway?

But check out this incredible insight to how vital God's presence is to the way we lead worship:

> The Levites who went far from me when Israel went astray and who wandered from me after their idols must bear the consequences of their sin. They may serve in my sanctuary, having charge of the gates of the temple and serving in it; they may slaughter

the burnt offerings and sacrifices for the people and stand before the people and serve them. But because they served them in the presence of their idols and made the people of Israel fall into sin, therefore I have sworn with uplifted hand that they must bear the consequences of their sin, declares the Sovereign LORD. They are not to come near to serve me as priests or come near any of my holy things or my most holy offerings; they must bear the shame of their detestable practices. And I will appoint them to guard the temple for all the work that is to be done in it.

But the Levitical priests, who are descendants of Zadok and who guarded my sanctuary when the Israelites went astray from me, are to come near to minister before me; they are to stand before me to offer sacrifices of fat and blood, declares the Sovereign LORD. They alone are to enter my sanctuary; they alone are to come near my table to minister before me and serve me as guards. (vv. 10–16)

Remember back when I mentioned the three-part calling of a Levite, described in Deuteronomy 10:8? Here's a great example of what happens when you miss honoring the presence of the Lord. Essentially, there were priests within the Levite tribe who were leading God's people astray to worship idols, and there had to be a penalty for their sin. God basically excommunicated these priests and revoked the sacred honor of ministering to Him. They could serve only as temple caretakers and do the "scrub work" of the temple.

It's very easy for us to slip from "presence mode" to "performance mode" and lead people astray. Are we inviting people to worship God or to worship us and our gifting? If it is the latter, then I'm afraid we may suffer the same consequence as these priests in Ezekiel 44. God still let them do work in His temple, but He wouldn't allow them to enjoy the greatest byproduct of worship, His presence. It's amazing to me that God had the grace to let these guys still serve. However, the sustaining love and joy that we find only in God's presence was taken from them.

One of my biggest fears as a leader is getting to a place where I rely on my ability more than I rely on the Holy Spirit. Now, this isn't a concrete theological thought, but from what I read in Ezekiel 44, I suppose God might still allow me to lead His people, but I wouldn't get to experience the joy found in ministering to Him. The very purpose of worship could be stripped away from us if we were to make the same mistake that these Old Testament priests made.

There was, however, one line of priesthood that remained steadfast in their worship, even when everyone else was losing their way. The priests of Zadok never lost sight of the true God among a land full of false ones. They continued to minister *faithfully* in the temple. So these were the only guys God would allow to continue ministering to Him. They were the only line of priests who could stand in His holy presence. My prayer is that we would always find ourselves identifying more with the line of Zadok than with the rest of the Levites, who led people down the wrong path.

The phrase "continued to minister faithfully" is what strikes me the most from this chapter. When everyone in our generation is screaming, "Look out for number one," God is calling us to make

Him the Lord of all. If we're always looking for the next best thing and believing that the grass is always greener in another pasture, then we'll never walk faithfully in the place that God has called us to.

Heather closed out her message to our team with a challenge that I'm still chewing on. She said, "Our role is also to experience the presence of Jesus. And we have a choice. We can minister to the people out of our own strength, or we can focus first on being in the presence of God and allow our ministry to the people to flow out of that."

Choose wisely. I never want to get to the point where I am more concerned about my performance than God's presence. Our passion for Jesus dies the moment we prefer creating our own show over ushering in His presence. If we continue to minister faithfully, as the line of Zadok did, we'll be able to continuously experience the goodness of His presence and the harvest that comes with it.

Make time for God's presence in your life. Start out your day in the Bible, prayer, worship, and whatever else you can do to move yourself into His presence. Authenticity happens when worship becomes a lifestyle and not just a set of songs that you lead for a half hour once a week. *The world doesn't need more great messages, more great bands, or even more great church services. We need more of God's presence.* Every move of revival is rooted in His presence. As authentic worship leaders, we need to be constantly refilling ourselves with God's Spirit, in His presence. If we're doing our job as worship leaders effectively, then we should be emptying ourselves every time we step into a place of leading worship. And when something is empty, it needs to be filled back up again. Otherwise you just become that scarecrow on stage, an empty shell going through the motions.

I attended the National Worship Leader Conference a couple of years ago and had the chance to hear Vaughn Thompson speak on leading as a servant. He said that the worship leader's position should be the lowest place in the room, because by the point you reach the weekend church service, it shouldn't be about the worship leader having his or her personal experience with God. It needs to be about connecting the congregation to the presence of God. It needs to be about bringing people to the awareness of how awesome God is!

One of the earliest worship leader "job descriptions" I heard as a teenager was "someone who ushers people into God's presence." Think about that for a second. Have you ever ushered at a wedding? The usher isn't the one sitting in on the wedding to enjoy the ceremony. Rather, the usher takes people to where they are supposed to be seated. The usher helps people find their place! That'll preach.

KNOW WHO YOU ARE

Nowadays, when you go to a big concert, you rarely see the actual headlining band go out and do its own sound check. They have roadies, guitar techs, and engineers who do all that legwork for them so they're able to focus on the big show and not worry about that "minor stuff." I can remember back to when my band had the chance to play a big festival and the guys running sound offered to check our instruments. Well, of course we wanted to be cool and have them take care of the sound check. I mean, who wouldn't? The only problem was, they didn't know our rig, and we ended up getting quite a bit of feedback and other monitor problems throughout the set. My point is, only *you* and God know your true sound. You can't live off someone else's authenticity, just like you can't live off another's faith. As my drummer friend Rico Allen once told me, "God doesn't have any grandchildren."

When I lead worship, I'm really the only one who knows how loud I'll sing into the mic or which frequencies my voice peaks at. So if I ask someone else to check the sound for me, I'm probably going to run into a few hiccups. In our lives, we know the areas that are blind spots, red flags, or problem zones.

Honesty is one of the most important parts of authenticity. Be real with who you are. When it comes to your worship team, if you have four people on the team, don't try to be a twenty-piece rock symphony. Be the best version of whatever team God has given you stewardship over. I look back on those early days leading worship at the church my dad pastored, when the worship team was a family band with just three of us on stage. I'm so grateful for those times. In fact, there are moments now when I miss the simplicity of that setup. Even though we had only a trio, we made every song count and did our very best every week to offer up a sound of worship that pleased God's heart and brought people closer to Him.

At NCC, with eight different campuses, we have eight unique bands, each with a sound that is authentic to their community. We have locations in the heart of the city as well as in the suburbs. We have bands that sound like the latest synth-rock group and bands that would make Stevie Wonder proud. It always keeps me on my toes as I try my best to get to every location at different times through-out the year to plug in to what is happening among our campuses. There is a ton of diversity within the different congregations and, as a reflection of that, within our worship teams. We don't want our different expressions of church to look like clones, but we do want to have a consistent quality across the board.

Many weeks, there are quite a few instrumentation gaps in the bands we have. Hey, it's hard to fill eight bands every weekend! We've learned that if you *show* your gaps, people will step up and ask about joining the worship team. However, if we just did a mad scramble every time we saw an open space in the schedule, we might never have anyone come up and ask how to join the team—they would assume we always have our positions covered.

Part of being authentic as a worship team is vulnerability, which comes out in full force when you expose your gaps. Recently, our Barracks Row worship leader, Chris Douglas, led worship from bass because they didn't have any bass players. It was a vulnerable move, but it paid off when two or three guys came to him at the end of the service and asked if they were looking for bassists. I'd say about half of our drummers are on our team because they simply asked, "Do you guys need more drummers here?" And every worship leader said yes and amen.

KNOW WHO YOU'RE NOT

Okay, I have a confession to make. There are literally two types of TV that I watch—sports and reality TV. One particular reality TV show might be one of the dumbest concepts out there, but I can't get enough of it. It's a show based in a pawnshop and follows three family members and staff as they run the shop. They buy and sell random antiques, artwork, and memorabilia that enter the store. Every now and then, an item comes in that's signed by a famous actor, sports star, or musician. Without fail, the head honcho always calls up one of his trusted friends to come and *authenticate* the signature. It's amazing how many forged signatures exist out there. If the autographed items are the real deal, they receive a certificate of authenticity, and they can be quite valuable. However, if the John Hancock turns out to be fake, it's not worth anything. In fact, if an item has a fake signature, it actually loses value. And trust me, if it's counterfeit, it will always be exposed.

You can see where this is heading. I wonder how many "forged copies" of true worship exist out there? Are we just imitating others and skating by on the faith and passion of those we admire? Or are we pushing ourselves to the limits of our own faith and seeking God with our whole hearts?

Sometimes as worship leaders, just as in any other occupation, it can be easy to hit "autopilot" and cruise through weeks, even months, without anyone (except ourselves) knowing the difference. We can pick the right songs, play the right transitions, and even say the right words in a worship setting (of course, you have to switch to your "prayer voice"—you know what I'm talking about). It's sad, but in most "forged" settings, people would rarely notice that something is off. That's when the authenticator comes in. As in the TV show I described, the authenticator puts the signatures under the microscope. The expert studies every curve and nuance of an autograph to tell if it's real or fake. Nothing escapes the authenticator's eyes.

In Luke 8:17, we see a picture of the great Authenticator: "For there is nothing hidden that will not be disclosed, and nothing

concealed that will not be known or brought out into the open."
God sees all, knows all, and deserves all. Who we are in the unseen
places of our lives will tell more about us than anything seen on a
stage. If you want to live an authentic life, you have to be who you
are, wherever you are. If I can only love people and lead them to
Christ with a microphone in front of me, I'm living a lie. I'd be com-
mitting forgery in my walk with Jesus. I recently had a conversation
with a local worship leader who said he was striving to lead worship
two hours at home for every hour he was on stage. I'm sure his wife
loves the at-home concerts!

Long before David was ever invited to play in the palace before
kings, he was playing in the pastures before the King of Kings. In
the latter half of 1 Samuel 16, we read that David's reputation as
an excellent musician was how he found himself playing his Fender
Harpocaster for King Saul. It's widely believed that David wrote
some of his most popular songs, including Psalm 23, in the lonely
hours of watching his flocks out in the fields, where there were no
spectators, no crowds screaming his name, and only the audience
of One. I would say that David's authenticity was a key reason God
anointed him for greatness. And that anointing took him from a
stump in a field to the throne of Israel.

When we live a worshipful life with no one watching, authenticity will come naturally when everyone is watching. Worship when
no one is around. Sing in your car, pray in the mornings, and see
a genuine life begin to manifest. God values the real deal and sees
when we are faking it. As in the TV show, forgeries are worthless.

One of the hardest struggles I have is whenever I'm at a church
service and *not* leading the worship. Talk about sound checking your

heart! I am constantly picking apart every musical note and transition that's happening on stage, taking notes, and thinking of how I would've done things differently. Often in my own pride, I consider how I could've done the songs better. I really got convicted of this a few years back when I was visiting family out of town and we went to their church for a Sunday morning service. The praise band was passionately leading the congregation in worship, and instead of joining in with their beautiful love offering to Jesus, all I could hear were musical mistakes and slightly off-pitch singing. How dare I scrutinize something so pure and holy to the Lord! I couldn't believe my own heart. In a repentant state, I made the choice to engage in worship and stop being the "worship music judge," because truth be told, no one needed my opinion anyway, certainly not God.

Recently, I had a conversation with one of our volunteer worship leaders and challenged him to be a worship leader from the congregation on the Sundays he wasn't leading on stage. Every time I saw him in a service that he wasn't playing, he just seemed to be standing in the crowd with a blank stare, arms folded, spectating rather than participating in the active worship of God. Then on the flip side, every time he was in the band on stage, he went all out with intense energy, wearing the biggest smile you'd ever seen. It seemed like a double life of worship.

How can we exhort our church body to lift their hands in praise and sing out to God with everything they have if we stand cross armed and disengaged in any services that we're not leading? I've gotten to serve with many amazing worshippers and leaders throughout the years, and one of my main dudes is a drummer friend, Bryan (from the click story). He has such passion for worship and always

CHECK YOUR PURPOSE   153

brings the sauce on the drums by playing with his whole heart. One of the things I love best about him actually comes in the moments he's not playing a beat. Whenever there's a down section in a song when the drums drop out, I can always look back and see Bryan with both arms raised to heaven, worshipping with everything he's got. That's authenticity!

We have to realize that whether we're on stage with an instrument or in the church rows singing, our call as worship leaders doesn't change. We can lead others in worship by praising on the frontlines, even when we're not mic'd up. This is why you can always tell the worship temperature of a church by seeing what a pastor does in the worship service. I've noticed that when a lead pastor isn't engaged during worship—or worse, not even physically present—typically the congregation is pretty unresponsive. However, if the lead pastor is immersed in passionate praise and going after God's presence with a heart of worship from the frontlines, it sets the tone for the whole church to respond. So the next service you attend and you're not leading the music, don't let that dictate the passion you bring to worshipping God. That's what makes an authentic worship leader.

My dad was a dairy farmhand back in his teenage years. Stories and metaphors from those days would often emerge in the messages he preached over his ten years as a pastor. One of his parables involved the whitewashed walls of a dairy farm. Every few years, farmhands have to paint over all the cow mess that has accumulated on the walls. Instead of scraping off the layers of poo and other nasty substances, a nice coat of white paint makes the walls look like new, at least for a little while. Worship leaders who live authentic lives after God are those who deal with the junk in their lives instead of stacking a ton of activities and accolades on top of a very messy reality. If you want to be the real deal, you have to deal with the real.

LOVE WORSHIP

Musical worship is not merely a warm-up to the pastor's message. Worship *is* a message! Not only does it send a message to God, but it also sends a warning to the enemy. It sends a declaration to our problems and to our circumstances that we're walking through. Take a look at 2 Chronicles 20, and read the story of Jehoshaphat's army heading into battle with their praise band on the frontlines. Can you imagine getting that phone call? "Yeah, we're heading to war, and we're gonna need you to grab your acoustic guitar and lead the charge!" I would've pulled a sick day. Not only did Israel win that war, but the three nations that came to fight against them that day, after hearing the sound of praise, actually turned on one another until every single soldier was dead. Verse 23 says, "The Ammonites and Moabites rose up against the men from Mount Seir to destroy and annihilate them. After they finished slaughtering the men from Seir, they helped to destroy one another."

I love this verse because my takeaway is that when we praise God and fix our eyes on Him, our problems take care of themselves. When we turn our attention to Jesus and how good He is, we quickly forget how overwhelming our problems can be. I had a firsthand experience with this a few years back when Sarah and I were the guest worship leaders for a youth group at a church about an hour outside of DC. (Yes, my wife is a worshipper. She even has a hot-pink bass.

It was awesome to see her rocking the bass and singing harmonies while thirty-eight-weeks pregnant with our daughter!)

But as we were driving there, we got into a disagreement, which escalated into an argument. I can't even remember what we were arguing about, but it was one of those epic "husband versus wife" battles that neither one of us wanted to lose. When we pulled up to the church, we decided to put our fight on pause and do what we came to do—lead worship. We may not have been in the right frame of mind when we walked into that church, but the moment we started to lift up songs of praise and worship God, something shifted in the atmosphere, and we ended up having a powerful encounter with His presence.

After the service, we got back into our car and laughed out loud, trying to remember what we had been fighting about. We ended up having an awesome conversation about worship on the way home and enjoyed the rest of the night. Thankfully, God can use imperfect people to do His perfect will. I'm grateful that He still chooses to use us, even when we are at our lowest points. Hey, if God spoke through a burning bush and even a donkey, then why not us?

To be an authentic worship leader, we have to understand the power behind what we're doing. If you just want to lead songs, then you should join a cover band. If you want to lead people into their eternal calling, then worship is where it's at!

Musical worship is no joke. If it were, we wouldn't have the Psalms, a book of 150 songs that have stood the test of time and hit every single feeling within humanity's scope of emotion. (I bet David and the other psalmists are wondering where their royalty checks are, considering modern-day worship songs pull many of their lyrics from the Psalms.)

Paul and Silas knew the value of worship. When they were imprisoned, they didn't let a jail cell stop them from praising: "About midnight Paul and Silas were praying and singing hymns to God, and the other prisoners were listening to them. Suddenly there was such a violent earthquake that the foundations of the prison were shaken. At once all the prison doors flew open, and everyone's chains came loose" (Acts 16:25–26). Chains are still breaking today every time the church lifts its song of praise to God.

In many of our church services, music is the introductory piece. For a person who is walking into church for the very first time, it could be his or her first idea of why the church exists and who God is. If that doesn't put a responsibility on us, I don't know what will. This demands that we show up with our best—our best abilities and our best selves—every time. The songs we sing in a worship service become the soundtrack to our church's conversation with the Father.

Worship is a gift from God's hand that connects us to His heart. To lead worship is something sacred that we should treat with the utmost honor and respect, because it *is* a gift from God. I love what God told Aaron and the Levites in Numbers 18:7: "And you and your sons with you shall guard your priesthood for all that concerns the altar and that is within the veil; and you shall serve. I give your priesthood as a gift, and any outsider who comes near shall be put to death" (ESV).

God didn't allow just anyone to serve Him in the sanctuary. In this Old Testament time period, anyone who approached the holy throne without the priesthood calling of a Levite would be killed! Thank God for the new covenant covering of Christ and His atoning grace—we don't face a death sentence for approaching Him in our humanity. In fact, Hebrews 4:16 spells out just how much the work of the cross matters in this context: "Let us then approach God's throne of grace with confidence, so that we may receive mercy and find grace to help us in our time of need."

God tells His ministers to guard their calling. How many of us regard our calling as sacred and lead worship with a sense of reverence? Have we become so familiar with Christ that we've lost our sense of awe and wonder for worship? Despite what some T-shirts might suggest, Jesus isn't your homeboy—He's your Savior. He has given those called to lead worship a special gift to guard wholeheartedly. It's a gift to cover in prayer.

Worship is prayer put to melody. For our worship to be most real, we have to allow for those moments when we pull back from the mic and allow our congregation to sing their own song, to offer up the prayers from their hearts. If the only lyrics we sing to God are those off a screen, it's about as authentic as me only telling my wife I love her by handing her a Hallmark card on Valentine's Day. When we realize the importance of praise, understanding the privilege it is to lead worship, we can more authentically lead our church. It all comes back to our heart. We don't worship God like we should because we don't love Him like we should. And we don't love Him like we should because we don't know Him like we should.

LOVE GOD

I appreciate how Bob and Larry define worship on the VeggieTales worship album: "Worship is when you do something that shows God how much you love Him." So then the question becomes, how should we love God? Moses said in Deuteronomy 6, and Jesus later said in Luke 10:27, "Love the Lord your God with all your heart, soul, mind, and strength." I also take this as a directive on how to worship God—with heart, soul, mind, and strength. Do we live our lives completely surrendered to God? Love is surrender. When I asked Sarah to marry me, I essentially said good-bye to the single, carefree, selfish way of life I was living. I surrendered the bachelor life to find something far more exciting, unpredictable, and fulfilling. That surrender has now been a ten-year adventure with my wife, made more exciting and crazier with two awesome kids. And I know the best is yet to come. None of the past ten years would have happened the way they did without the initial surrender.

Love is at the core of authenticity. Jesus was the epitome of love and authenticity. He lived a life of sacrifice and service, leading and loving others in a way the world had never seen before and hasn't truly seen since. He loved His heavenly Father above everything else and placed His Father's will above His own. As worship leaders, *our call to love God is higher than anything else.* When we love God, we'll lead others to Him naturally. My desire in leading worship isn't simply to *point* people to Jesus but to *lead* people straight to Him. The New Testament presents worship leaders with two great examples on how to love God with our ministry. The first is the classic story of Mary and Martha:

> As Jesus and his disciples were on their way, he came
> to a village where a woman named Martha opened
> her home to him. She had a sister called Mary, who
> sat at the Lord's feet listening to what he said. But

Martha was distracted by all the preparations that had to be made. She came to him and asked, "Lord, don't you care that my sister has left me to do the work by myself? Tell her to help me!"

"Martha, Martha," the Lord answered, "you are worried and upset about many things, but few things are needed—or indeed only one. Mary has chosen what is better, and it will not be taken away from her." (Luke 10:38–42)

Martha was preoccupied with doing things *for* Jesus, whereas Mary was more interested in being *with* Jesus. They were both done out of love, but Jesus said that Mary's approach was better. A major part of loving someone is just being *with* that person. I can say I'm in love with my wife, but if I'm never present, then it's going to be hard to convince her that my love is real. At the end of the day, my wife doesn't want to see all the things I can do for her—she just wants me. That was what Jesus was relaying in Luke 10. Sometimes leaders can get so caught up in doing things *for* God that we forget the call to just be *with* Him. As Corrie ten Boom once said, "If the Devil can't make us bad, he'll make us busy."

Back before my daughter was obsessed with *Frozen* and many other princess movies, she was into very simple toys. Trust me, Norah has a nice collection to choose from, thanks to generous grandparents. In her first year of life, our living-room floor was usually covered with *Sesame Street* characters and all sorts of blocks and cars. (Funny thing is, Norah would be just as content playing with one of her socks—having that knowledge before her first Christmas would've saved us a lot of coin.) On one particular morning, instead of pulling out all of her toys, I decided to just take out a little Nerf basketball we had been playing with for a couple of weeks. She absolutely loved that cheap piece of foam. In her simple joy of playing with that ball, I realized something interesting: When she had a ton of toys strewn all across the floor, she would usually ignore all of them and crawl away bored. However, if there was just the *one* item out to play with, she'd spend at least ten minutes with it, having a great time.

Why do I say all of this? It's about distractions. Think of the Nerf basketball as Christ, and envision all those toys scattered across the floor as the things that crowd our busy lives. Those distractions include selfish dreams, wrong motives, entertainment, busyness, or anything else that can potentially take away the centered focus on Jesus. When you remove all that clutter and leave only Jesus, you find that He is more than enough to satisfy your soul. Every problem, every situation, every circumstance in our lives can be figured out with more of Jesus. He is the answer to our most pressing questions.

It's not just about *adding* great disciplines to our routine—reading the Bible, going to church, attending small groups, singing worship songs. It's also about what we are *subtracting*. Are we getting rid of those things that don't add value to our relationship with Christ? Authentic worship leaders know the things they must add to and subtract from their lives to be the genuine article.

The second example of how worship leaders can love God with our ministry comes from Matthew 26:

> While Jesus was in Bethany in the home of Simon
> the Leper, a woman came to him with an alabaster

jar of very expensive perfume, which she poured on his head as he was reclining at the table. When the disciples saw this, they were indignant. "Why this waste?" they asked. "This perfume could have been sold at a high price and the money given to the poor."

Aware of this, Jesus said to them, "Why are you bothering this woman? She has done a beautiful thing to me. The poor you will always have with you, but you will not always have me. When she poured this perfume on my body, she did it to prepare me for burial. Truly I tell you, wherever this gospel is preached throughout the world, what she has done will also be told, in memory of her." (vv. 6–13)

What the disciples saw as wasteful and pointless, Jesus called beautiful. He even said that her display of love and worship would be told wherever the gospel story went. Some accounts of this story mention that the woman here was a prostitute, which would've meant she wasn't a welcomed or invited guest. Yet she made her way to Jesus and poured every ounce of the precious perfume on Him. Matthew Henry's commentary on this passage says, "The pouring ointment upon the head of Christ was a token of the highest respect. Where there is true love in the heart to Jesus Christ, nothing will be thought too good to bestow upon him."

Love holds nothing back. Just as this woman poured every ounce of expensive fragrance on Jesus, we are called to pour every ounce of worship at His feet. This story was the inspiration behind a song I wrote with Joel Buckner called "You Alone." It's a love song telling

God that He alone deserves our worship and praise. Everything we are and all that we have belong to Him. Nothing and no one else are worthy of our devoted lives. A devoted life is an act of love. When we are fully devoted to God, we are able to lead worship and love others in the most genuine way. I have a simple tag line that I try to live by: "Love God. Love people. Write songs that show it."

I started off this book by telling you that most of my music journey has had two sides: Rock Band Kurtis and Worship Leader Kurtis. Recently, I was encouraged and prophesied over by a pastor that God isn't necessarily asking me to choose between these two courses, because He's given me both. I am a rock star in His eyes by leading worship for His church. Knowing my blind spots will keep me in line with His path for my life. I've got to be aware of the problem of pride and the white noise that surrounds us and distracts us from authenticity. I've learned to pay attention to the distractions in my life, because if I ignore them, I won't see them creeping up on me. And that's what makes distractions dangerous.

Know your blind spots as a leader. And if you find yourself continuously falling into the same traps, have other people you can trust tell you the truth when everyone else around you feeds you lies. You need people who will tell you what you *need* to hear, which won't always be what you *want* to hear. This also has a very practical application to us as worship leaders. If everyone in the room during a rehearsal never has a point of difference about the songs than you, then your songs will always sound the same. However, when you have around you people who think differently about music than you do, it would be a slap in the face of diversity not to open yourself up to others' opinions. Remember that when a band is sound checking, it's not the bandleader who makes the adjustments to the mix—it's the person behind the soundboard.

We need others to make us stronger and to help us in our lives by seeing what we don't necessarily see. My wife is great about this. I write and produce a lot of different music, and she has the "great fortune" of always being around when I get a mix back to listen to. I can always tell from the look on her face if a song needs adjustments. And I'll admit, she's pretty much always right. If I've heard a song fifty times, I get to a point where I might miss something here and there because I've gotten used to it. The song has become overly familiar to me. But when Sarah hears a song for the first time, she picks out parts that need tightening or a harmony that might be a little off. I guess I need to start listing her as coproducer on my projects.

We get accustomed to the same routines in our lives, and as worship leaders, that can be dangerous. We go with what we know and what's familiar. We take the safe route. But safe is never that much fun, because there isn't much challenge in safe. One of NCC's core values is "everything is an experiment." That value is awesome for anyone with a creative edge, because it gives us the permission to fail. Not 100 percent of my ideas will work in a worship setting. In fact, sometimes I fall flat on my face.

I was asked to lead worship at a conference a couple of years back, and I wanted to try something fresh with the worship set, because most of the songs I was leading were pretty familiar by that time. I'd also just started to mess around with a new synth keyboard that had some crazy effects on it. This was right around the same time that every pop song was throwing in that autotune and vocoder stuff, so I thought I'd try to bring a little T-Pain into our worship set. The only problem was, when we got to the song I was going to use the effect on, I forgot to switch the keyboard to vocoder mode and was singing into a microphone that never got turned on for about five straight seconds. If all had gone right, I'm sure it would've been one of the coolest music transitions we've ever done. But of course, all didn't go according to plan, and it made for one of the more awkward moments I've had on stage in recent memory. My friends who were there that day won't ever let me forget that moment, and it's been the source of quite a few jokes. But hey, at least I tried something new! For the record, I gave myself a second chance with the vocoder when we did an electronica worship night, and it was pretty sweet!

We all long for authenticity. The whole world is crying out for it. The church needs it! And God is searching for those authentic worshippers who will worship Him in Spirit and in truth. For far too long, I lived my life as a fake—looking like I had it all together on the outside while internally struggling to know who I was and where my worth came from. Between traveling in a rock band and leading worship, I was constantly battling pride and mostly losing the war.

You and I know that it's totally possible to lead worship in our own strength and maybe even to get away with it—for a while. It can be like the frog that is slowly being boiled in water but doesn't realize it until it's too late. We can all have an "off" Sunday or even a season when we don't sense the Lord in our quiet times. We shift into "autopilot" and continue to lead our churches in worship, maybe out of obedience … or maybe just because it's our job!

There can be many reasons for this. It may be that our focus has shifted off Jesus and onto ourselves. Maybe we're just getting a little too much significance from being upfront on stage. Maybe there's some hidden area of sin in our lives. Whatever the reason, if the condition is left unchecked, there can be a price to pay in terms of isolation, depression, fatigue, and burnout. There is also the effect on your church that comes from being led by an inauthentic worship leader.

If this is you, I'd like to encourage you to go to someone you trust (ideally your pastor) and share what's going on and ask for prayer. I know it's hard for leaders to do sometimes, because we're supposed have our acts together, right? The Bible is full of leaders who constantly messed up and yet were still used and transformed by God. We can be thankful that God doesn't always call the qualified, but He always qualifies the called! He is more concerned with who you *are* than what you can *do* for Him. So if this strikes a chord in you (forgive the pun), let Him minister and bring healing to that hurting or needy place in your soul. You may even need a "time-out" from your leadership role for a season. If so, you will come out on the other side more aware of your daily need for a Savior ... and you won't be faking leading worship anymore. You will, in fact, be on the road to becoming an authentic worship leader.

I love the phrase used by my friend Simon Dixon, who contributed many thoughts to this chapter: "God often transforms us on the go." Scripture assures us that we are being transformed into His image with ever-increasing glory (2 Cor. 3:18). None of us have arrived, and as long as we are on this earth, we never will fully arrive. But that's the amazing part of a life in Christ. There's always another level to step into. Let this be your reassurance that God can change us while we are in process. He doesn't need perfect people to carry out His perfect will. He promises to supply our every need, and that includes everything we need to live our lives in authentic worship. Be who you are, and let God be who He is.

We know that God is looking for a generation of genuine worshippers and worship leaders. John 4:24 tells us that. This whole book has been a challenge and an encouragement to worship leaders and church leaders who want to live with authenticity. And when your search leads to Jesus, you don't need to look any further. Jesus is authenticity to the core.

The dictionary defines the word *true* as "real, genuine, or authentic." To be true worship leaders and real followers of Christ, we need to go after *the truth*. As Jesus says, "I am the way and the truth and the life. No one comes to the Father except through me" (John 14:6). Jesus's arms are always open wide, and He's never been an exclusive Savior. He invites us all into an absolutely real relationship. That relationship is to be the foundation of everything we do in our lives. Leading our families, teams, and churches in authentic worship can happen only when we allow ourselves to be led by the One who gave His life for us.

This book isn't meant to tell you who you are. It's intended to be a nudge to go find out who you are through the power of the Holy Spirit in God's presence. Never stop seeking Him. Never let Him stop tuning you. He will remove all of the noise and feedback. He will leave only the most accurate and beautiful sound that is pleasing to His ears. Never stop sound checking.

Testing … testing … one, two, three.

CHECK YOUR PURPOSE   167

FOR GROUP DISCUSSION OR PERSONAL REFLECTION

1. How can you keep a heart for God's presence while still maintaining a spirit of excellence (not getting lost in performance)?

2. What are three unique qualities that your team possesses?

3. What do you need to *subtract* from your daily life in order to *add* a higher focus on God's calling?

BIBLE CREDITS

KURTIS IS PASSIONATE ABOUT CONNECTING WITH CHURCHES AND MINISTRIES!

TO BOOK KURTIS TO COME AND SPEAK OR LEAD WORSHIP, PLEASE VISIT WWW.KURTISPARKS.COM